Where individuals are
required to be strong & selfless,
I stand by them. Where individuals
give more love than they receive
back, I stand close by. Where
people need the inspiration to
complete remarkable lives,
I offer my help. I am
close to you and wait your
invitation to give you so much.

Lord Sananda / Lord Jesus.

Ascension

Becoming an Ascended Master

Paul McCarthy

iUniverse, Inc.
Bloomington

iUniverse books may be ordered through booksellers or by contacting:

iUniverse
1663 Liberty Drive
Bloomington, IN 47403
www.iuniverse.com
1-800-Authors (1-800-288-4677)

ISBN: 978-1-4502-7380-0 (sc)
ISBN: 978-1-4502-7381-7 (hc)
ISBN: 978-1-4502-7382-4 (ebook)

Printed in the United States of America

iUniverse rev. date: 01/05/2011

To contact the Author

You can contact the author by email at:

guidedbythelight@hotmail.com

Website: siriusascension.com

Contents

Introduction   1

What is and Ascension and an Ascended Master?!   7

How to transcend the negative ego   17

Who Am I? Identification   29

Ascension Integration   33

Advanced Ascension ways of being   40

Universal Awareness   45

A Model of Ascension   56

Indigo Consciousness - Intellectual Exploration   63

Crystal Consciousness - Emotional Exploration   73

Rainbow Consciousness - Multidimensional Exploration   88

Diamond Consciousness - Divine Exploration and
Expression   96

Introduction

Throughout the ages many have sought to achieve the ultimate goal of spiritual growth and experience. This is Ascension, the climax and conclusion of human spiritual growth and evolved human consciousness. Some have failed and yet many still continue down this path attracted by the promise of a mystical union with the Divine that is both unimaginable and profound. This inner calling is strong and for some Ascension becomes their main focus in life. I call such souls the *Ascension Seekers* and this book is dedicated to these brave and ambitious individuals. If you have found your way to this book then you too are probably an Ascension Seeker.

The awareness of Ascension has been present amongst spiritual seekers for a long time. There have been many ideas about what Ascension actually is. There have been different descriptions and definitions used throughput the ages. These reflected the cultures of specific times as well as the awareness of those exploring spirituality at that time. Ascension has been viewed as the path to freedom from the earthly cycles of lifetimes, the journey to become a spiritual master and the mystical union with the light (divine energy and consciousness). These are all part of the process of ascension and yet there is a more expanded understanding which is that to ascend is to transform our consciousness itself from lower consciousness (human) to higher consciousness (Universal or Divine). For many years this was considered the only goal of ascension. The popular assumption was that when we ascend we depart the physical world in a literal flash of light. Interestingly this popular view reveals much about the level of consciousness of ascension seekers of that period which in my view ended in the years 2000-2003. It shows that a major motivation for some was to escape this harsh world where ascension became a personal route out of the lower consciousness of humanity. However the current generation of ascension seekers have come to terms with the negativity of humanity and now wish to define ascension in different ways by asking, "What follows my Ascension"? The question implies that following ascension an individual remains on earth. The growing realisation is that ascension seekers are to ascend and then to embody and express Divine Consciousness in this world. This invariably leads ascension seekers to helping others (service work). This is the expanded definition of Ascension.

One who has achieved Ascension is called an Ascended Master. This term conjures images of past Spiritual Masters such as Jesus Christ and Buddha. For many it is inconceivable to imagine that they too will experience Ascension like those Ascended Masters who came before them. And yet this is their destiny in this New Golden Age which offers unrivalled opportunity for personal spiritual growth as the universal flow of spiritual energies and consciousness strongly supports this theme.

There are those who are seduced by the perceived glamour of the spiritual skills of Ascended Masters and by their desire for recognition from others. These are not the right motivations for Ascension and anyone seeking such things will probably be disappointed as such desires will undermine their own efforts.

And so what is the flavour of Ascension in this modern world? Are these new Ascended Masters to be like those of the past? Are they to be the evangelists and outspoken teachers of the past? Are they to give miraculous healings and form new spiritual groups or even new religions? No, the requirement of the modern age is to be a service worker which is someone one who is dedicated to helping humanity in whatever ways that they can. Sometimes this can be in hidden or less obvious forms of assistance than we assume an Ascended Master would participate in. The expression "there are many Masters amongst us" describes this reality. The mission is to open the hearts of men and women which will lead to the ascension of consciousness in humanity itself. It is through the Heart that we find higher consciousness. It is the destiny of humanity in general to raise its consciousness to the Crystal level which is the way of the Heart. The mission is also to empower others by showing them their true potential as human beings and as spiritual beings. This is achieved not through creating more religions, organisations and hierarchies. It is achieved by showing people their own abilities to connect to spiritual realities by themselves. This is the path to freedom and higher consciousness.

What lies ahead for us individually and collectively is beyond the imagination of most and yet we can begin to see its effect now as I will describe. However the truth is that this is a time of great potentials and not of fixed destinies. As such the actual experience of this time is being co-created by us individually and collectively.

Having facilitated over sixty spiritual workshops worldwide from over the last five years, I have witnessed the profound transformation in consciousness in hundreds of the workshop participants. I have regularly worked with most of them and so I am able to see their progression and in some cases individuals have evolved to the next higher band of human spiritual consciousness in only two to five years. Some have continued into even higher bands of consciousness. This level of progression in human spiritual consciousness has not been seen for a long time. Personal evolution is truly their reality and they represent the living proof of what is available to so many.

But it is hard. It is the nature of ALL human beings to resist change and especially if this means accepting that their thoughts or behaviour are no longer appropriate for their needs. At a mundane level people find it hard to embrace new habits and yet there is more to this than merely the mundane. At the core of all resistance is fear. This is not the instinctive and physical fear of our survival mechanism. I am talking about the ego's fear which at a deep sub-conscious level it knows that it is living on borrowed time. Inside all of us there is an awareness of what we were before we developed the ego as a condition of being a human being. The ego is of course a temporary illusion in which we believe that "I" is an individual being separate from all other beings and indeed "I" is separate from Source/God/Oneness. Buried deep inside of us is the truth that we are spirit having a human experience which is only temporary and that we will return back to that full state of being. The ego in all of us is working hard to maintain its existence and the ascension process is fundamentally the way of dismantling the ego sufficiently enough so that the soul and spirit can be expressed in our human experience.

As I write these words the realities of an expanding awareness in the western world is evident. The lies, greed and corruption are being exposed within the worlds of business, religion and politics may come as a surprise to many. This is however a sign that humanity's awareness is growing. The ability to differentiate between lies and illusions from truth is an aspect of higher consciousness. This is an important and significant achievement in the ascension of humanity.

The collective consciousness is no longer so asleep that the religious, political and the business communities can exploit humanity to the same degree as in the past. Although the use of lies, fear and misinformation may continue they will not influence so many as before nor will their impact be felt as deeply. From a spiritual perspective you could say the current spiritual energies and themes support global revelation and illumination and work towards highlighting all negativity that is committed against humanity.

Of course this book reflects my own experience of my own Ascension. I have created an in depth model and map of Ascension for others to use on their journey in order that their experience of Ascension is more illuminated and empowered. In using this model and my teachings of Ascension I can see how it applies to the many Ascension Seekers that I have met in my workshops that I have given all around the world.

I have presented this subject in a way that is largely free of new age technical jargon, religious and ancient mystical references. By doing this I hope to allow this subject to be more accessible to those who do not necessarily have a background in spiritual theory. However the study of personal consciousness does require an ability to be aware of one's own thoughts and emotions. This is what I write about and therefore the reader is encouraged to be aware of these aspects of self in order to apply the material to their own life and spiritual growth.

There are many approaches that a writer of ascension can take. This book is a guide to the journey through different levels of consciousness that is ascension. I have written it because I meet so many spiritual seekers who recognise that they are experiencing spiritual transformation but they are unaware of where they are placed within the process. They also do not know how to navigate the twists and turns in a graceful way leading to the next level. Very often they find themselves confused and trapped within patterns of growth as they cannot complete the core spiritual requirements needed to be worked on in order to free themselves of these patterns. I have yet to find a model of ascension that is complete, easily accessible to a western reader and written in modern terms. As such I have created a model of ascension that explains in detail the experiences of each level of ascension, the unique lessons of each level as well as the requirements needed to take them to the next level. This book is a guide to the process and journey of ascension. It does not describe the beauty and profundity of ascension and I would like to dedicate another book to that approach. However the need for a map is urgent and important and I hope this book contributes to that effort.

An important contribution of the book is to draw the reader to the energy of the book which surrounds every copy that will be eventually be printed. All books connect the reader to the energetic field consciousness of the author. In the case of this book the energies will speak to you at different levels of your being reflecting the interactive nature and the oneness of Universal Awareness. If you take a moment to connect to the energy whilst holding the book you may notice this. It is the nature of a Master to be able to notice such things and read the energies of all things. Of course an author writes from their own level of consciousness and with the subject of ascension this is especially important to appreciate when reading writing about ascension. I have seen books that reflect the nature of the Indigo and Crystal levels but rarely the Rainbow and Diamond levels. This means that all spiritual seekers must be discerning about what they read and ingest from those claiming to be knowledgeable in this area or indeed from those on earth who claim to be ascended masters themselves.

I write about Universal Consciousness and Universal Awareness. This has the same meaning as Spirit, The I AM Presence and The Monad. These words are interchangeable. In a similar way when I refer to the Universe I refer to the totality of that which has been created including the collective intelligence, love and purpose of all that is. You can also use the words Source and God. They are interchangeable. For those who relate to Angels and Guides then again although I do not refer to them directly, these can be taken to be the voices and agents of the Divine.

What is and Ascension and an Ascended Master?!

Ascension

It is the deliberate expansion and refinement of personal consciousness. Spiritual growth is the route for this and here I include personal psychological, emotional and energetic mastery too. Energetic mastery refers to the development, evolution, understanding and skilled interaction with our energetic bodies. These include our auras, chakras, light bodies and many forms of spiritual energies such as healing energies and the Rays. At a higher level Ascension is the experience of merging with oneness / light / God after letting go of the identification of the human personality and ego.

The complete achievement of ascension results in a level of personal mastery of all aspect's of self from the human perspective. These include:

Transcendence of the negative ego - This is the recognition and removal of the illusionary identity of self as a separate being. This includes the negative and limited thoughts and feelings at the conscious and sub-conscious levels. This process includes the transformation of negative thoughts, emotions and energies.

The positive movement away from ego thinking towards spiritual oneness - Oneness is the identification with the reality that we are connected to everything through source / God. Through an expanded awareness and the thorough exploration of spiritual realities we recognise and embrace this oneness which already exists.

Integration - the completion and healing of unresolved aspects of past lives and karmic issues leading to the completion of all the cycles of earthly incarnations of growth patterns, karma and service work. These unresolved aspects of past lives are usually emotional and energetic problems that were not able to be healed in the relevant lifetime and follow us to the current lifetime. These could be emotional problems such as trauma, abandonment or despair. They could include energetic problems such as energy bocks within chakras. Limited and negative belief patterns from past lives can also be present themselves, often working from the sub-conscious mind and influencing our current reality.

Integration also includes the awareness and unification of all aspects of self. We are multi-dimensional beings with many aspects such as soul, spirit, chakras, sub-conscious mind, light bodies, aura, past lives, physical body and so forth. To be an Ascended Master is to not only be aware of these aspects of self but to skilfully bring them together so that they are working in alignment to serve our highest purpose. To be a master of self is to work with all aspects of self.

Being your higher self in daily life

Mastery is not just an intellectual appreciation of these things. It is the daily expression of them in everyday situations. Life itself brings all kinds of challenges where we are "tested". Here we may express higher or lower ways of responding to situations. These tests often highlight areas that we are working on or need to focus on. For example if we are working on claiming our personal power, then life presents challenges in the form of people who may try to take advantage of us or undermine us. We then have the perfect opportunity to speak our truth and express our personal power. These tests tend to recur until we have elevated ourselves away from those energies by learning our lessons and moving onto new subjects. We then do not attract those situations so much. There are octaves of these themes, lessons and growth opportunities. Here the higher octave shows us deeper insights into an area of spiritual development.

The actual experience of the process of Ascension is unique for everyone. We all have different lessons, skills and life missions on earth. Our Ascension is supported by the cosmic movement of energies and consciousness that has been taking place and reaches a climax in 2012. In this sense everyone is involved in the theme of Ascension by virtue of being on earth right now. The real question is are we resisting this or embracing this? These cosmic energies come to earth with great purpose and perfect timing. New energies are arriving all the time to help us move to the next level of ascension.

Enlightenment vs. Ascension

Enlightenment tends to refer to someone who has experienced significant spiritual growth. They could be considered to be wise and aligned to spiritual energies and the light. Most ascension seekers have experienced lifetimes where they have had opportunities to become somewhat enlightened. This is a big part of the ascension process but it is not the act of ascension itself. The aspect of ascension that makes it different is that ascension is the movement towards completing all earthly cycles such as karma, lessons and service work. Enlightenment does not necessarily include all of the things which are essential for ascension.

What is an ascended master?

> **"An ascended Master is a master of self and not anyone else."**

> **"An Ascended Master is a master of thought, emotion and energy. "**

An Ascended Master is a being who has ascended their personal consciousness and achieved mastery. Here mastery means the ability to be aware of all aspects of self and to consciously and skilfully be able to choose how to experience their reality. As much as is possible, a master chooses to only experience the highest personal thoughts, emotions and energies.

A Master has learnt the ability to attract what they desire into their lives. This is also called the manifestation process and can include specific people, opportunities and situations as well as more common things such as financial abundance.

A Master expresses his life missions with joy. They will have discovered their true purpose for being here and what it is that their soul would ideally experience in this lifetime. They will be able to greatly disconnect from the distractions and illusions that daily life offers so that they can concentrate on their life missions. They will understand their own unique gifts and how these can be shared with planet earth and mankind as a spiritual act of service. They will have aligned their acts of service with the broader plan for earth, working consciously or unconsciously (guided through intuition) alongside the Divine.

An expanded definition of an ascended master includes the recognition of the achievement of a high level of spiritual growth and expanded consciousness. This includes the transcendence of the negative ego and human condition. A Master demonstrates their higher consciousness in daily life through how they respond to challenges. This is much more than just an intellectual understanding of higher ways of being as it is the expression of these in the physical world.

A Master is somewhat integrated meaning that they are aware of different aspects of self such as life purpose, their personal spiritual energies, guides, past lives, soul essence and personal gifts. They will have also achieved a personal balance of polarities such as emotions / mind, male / female, physical / spiritual and doing / being. This balance is different for everyone as we are all unique in our mental, emotional and energetic makeup.

A Master has healed and cleared all aspects of self across all time and space. This allows that individual to be free to choose not to return to earth if this is their desire.

What is the Ego?

The ego is our sense of reality in which we are individuals and separate from other people and everything around us both in the seen world around us and in unseen spiritual realities. We need an ego in order to operate on earth. Without an ego we would not be able to get out of bed in the morning! The absence of an ego would mean that our consciousness would be greatly aware of the oneness of source / God. I doubt that in that blissful state we would be able to comprehend the reality that we were in a physical body which we alone control and which is separated physically from all the other physical things around us. This reality would be too bizarre to comprehend and we would simply be in the body without moving.

The Ego is not a new concept invented for physical living. In the spirit world where we exist in between lives, the soul energy exists with a sense of ego too. Each soul is created with a unique blend of spiritual energies, potentials and motivations. There is a sense of individuality about the soul energies. The soul has a comprehensive and personal awareness of these aspects and also memories of its full existence. At this level there is still an awareness of Source / God as well as the understanding that each soul is a part of Source / God. As such there is a sense of individuality as well as a sense of connection to everything else. This brings great meaning and purpose to the experience of the soul.

Our human experience on earth is very different. Our sense of individuality becomes distorted as it becomes exaggerated. We lose the sense of connection to source, other beings and even our own soul. Our sense of self becomes a reality where "I" exists in isolation away from everything else. Why does this happen? We are placed in a physical body whose predominant senses such as sight and hearing focus our attention away from our internal awareness of spiritual realities. We become too focused in the physical world where it is harder to recognise spiritual connection and realities. We live in a culture and at a time where society ignores spiritual realities and truth. We lose memories of the soul experience. This amnesia creates a vacuum where we search for meaning, direction and purpose. Something else emerges in this vacuum which is the negative ego.

The Negative Ego is a self-identity created from childhood whose fundamental view is that we are each separate from other people and from God. This is an illusion and is so convincing on earth that nearly everyone believes this to be true at the personality level. Of course those who have awoken spiritual recognise this illusion as we are all part of source and connected in energy and consciousness at all levels of our being. This illusion of a separated identity creates a lonely and difficult experience. It promotes fear and this brings about negative thoughts, emotions and energies. This is why it attracts the name "negative" ego as fundamentally it brings about negative experiences if it is allowed to influence a personality without restriction. This identity seeks to protect itself and its views. The negative ego distorts truth to serve its own aims. Hence there is usually a lack of mental clarity, integrity and truth with those greatly influenced by their negative egos. The expressions of this include pride, anger and arrogance. The negative ego brings a sense of satisfaction in self when it finds ways to justify its own agenda of being "right" and continuing its separated identity. This feels like a reward and convinces many that their negative thoughts and behaviour must be right. These feelings of being right are only temporary and so negative patterns continue indefinitely seeking further confirmations and justifications for its existence. There are no true feelings of unconditional love, joy and peace within this level of consciousness as these would threaten the existence of the negative ego. Many are trapped in this self-perpetuating cycle of negativity created by their own negative ego. It is only when the person becomes so tired of this negativity and surrenders to a higher spiritual power that they can begin to transcend the negative ego. Often this process is supported by the universe. Here life itself presents situations and opportunities for the individual to realise that it is time for transformation and that the pattern of denial and resistance cannot continue.

We all need to transcend the negative ego and fear as part of the process of surrender. The negative ego provides the most resistance to surrender. The main cause of resistance is fear of the unknown. It is a fear of change and a fear of loss of control that emanates from the negative ego. A negotiation is entered into at a sub-conscious level. How much will the negative ego allow us to surrender without resistance? The negative ego wants to avoid changing habits and thoughts and it enters into many negotiations with us at deep levels as it tries to avoid changes to our thoughts and habits. We feel this as reluctance to change even if this is best for us. Examples are a poor diet, lack of exercise, negative relationships, inappropriate job, an abuse of alcohol or any other stimulants such as cigarettes or coffee etc, unwillingness to forgive, grudges, anger, hurt, pain, negative opinions and thoughts. The negative ego persuades us that we can maintain these and still have spiritual growth. This is an illusion and we eventually see this. The negative ego uses fear and pain to signal to us to stop. This becomes a partial surrender which is where we understand something intellectually but we do not engage the emotions and a movement of energy in order to avoid our fear. This partial surrender is a false surrender. We may feel some relief with a false surrender as it appears to have avoided feeling pain. This is only a temporary situation as life will once again present the opportunities to re-visit the same growth patterns in an attempt to achieve full surrender. Surrender is therefore unconditional.

Through disciplined spiritual and psychological work it is possible to dismantle this distorted identity. This allows the soul level identity of oneness balanced with ego to be present at the personality level. This is called transcending the negative ego. When this is done the causes of negative thoughts and emotions are removed and unconditional love, joy, and peace are experienced. These are soul level experiences brought into our human experience. This process is the essential part of personal ascension.

What is beyond the transcendence of the negative ego?

Transcending the negative ego is only part of the ascension journey, as there needs to be a movement towards expanded consciousness and oneness that are not achieved through typical methods of working on the negative ego alone. I write about these in detail in the section called Advanced Ascension ways of being. By transcending the negative ego we allow ourselves the ability to see beyond normal human experience. The transcendence of the negative ego frees us to do the actual work of ascension. What lies beyond normal human experience? The answer is the divine with all of its different dimensions and mysteries! A movement towards oneness includes identifying with, merging with, aligning with, enjoying and exploring all aspects of the divine. This is the way of the heart / level of consciousness called Unconditional Love.

There is a tendency for a lot of new age ascension schools to place much of their focus on transcending the negative ego and not enough focus on embracing the divine. As such we find a lot of spiritual students becoming experts at spotting the negative ego in operation and yet they are devoid of any profound personal spiritual experiences or insights. There needs to be a balance of both focuses.

Integration

Integration is a big part of personal ascension. Each lifetime has the potential to contain incomplete lessons, experiences, relationships, missions and unresolved negative emotions. These "pull" you back to earth to complete and resolve and may build up the desire within your soul to reincarnate again. This is similar view to how many see the laws of Karma. However the move towards ascension is to resolve all these outstanding matters in this lifetime and complete the current cycle of lifetime so that we can move on to a new cycle of experience, service and growth. It is normally within the Indigo state of consciousness that we do most of this work. Here we are attracted to resolving relationships, healing, personal psychological work and emotional work of all kinds. These include inner child work, past life work, energetic work (healing, acupuncture etc) spiritual psychology (including the sub conscious mind), counselling and many other therapies.

Integration is also the process of being aware of different aspects of self and bringing them into harmony and aligning them together. For example we allow our soul to guide us in life. We make choices based on what our soul needs rather than what the personality alone desires. We experience existence through all lenses and not just a few. We balance emotions with thought, the needs of spirit with physical needs and balance service to self with service to others.

The Negative Ego and Self Love There is a lot of confusion about the relationship between the negative ego and self love. Some view the negative ego as a manmade thing that is undesirable and is to be rejected. Others view it as something that needs to be loved and integrated into our whole being.

The effects of having a negative ego are undoubtedly undesirable, as it is the source of most types of suffering. However the ego is constructed for a reason. Without the sense of self and individuality we would not be able to function in modern society or indeed the physical world. It is a necessity. Without it we would simply have no concept of being an individual in a physical body. We would simply experience oneness without any connection to the physical world. As such the ego is not a bad thing as we need some sense of individuality in order to function and survive. However where this sense of a separate self becomes so exaggerated that there is no room for any awareness of source, spirit or soul then this is a problem. At that level of ego domination there is little more than the suffering brought about by the negative ego.

We teach babies and children to quickly develop this sense of a separate self in order to protect them. As a society we teach them about fear in order that they do not get burnt or run in front of a car. Later on we expand this and try to protect their emotions and sense of identity. Unwittingly we become the architects of the negative ego. Ironically later on we then have to undo much of what has been created in terms of negative ego through a spiritual approach. As such no one should blame themselves because they have a negative ego. It is not their fault as it is a by-product of modern living. We need to love ourselves despite the fact that we have a negative ego. Through spiritual study many are exploring the workings and content of their negative ego. What they find may be disturbing, ugly and surprising. Their findings do not seem to reconcile with the image many of ourselves as being spiritual and loving. However it does not serve us to hate or fear our negative ego. Negative emotions will always create undesirable outcomes. Instead we can see the negative ego as a program that was installed in our childhood that we continued to develop in adulthood. It got carried away and now we have decided to re-program ourselves so that we can experience a higher way of being. There is no need for blame or regret. Please love yourself even though you have a negative ego! This does not mean that you should suffer at the hands of it but rather that a balanced sense of perspective is needed here. Being an Ascended Master means having transcended the negative ego. However you will still probably need some sense of self as an individual as well if you want to continue earthly living. There is a balance point where expanded consciousness and oneness can be achieved whilst still maintaining a physical body and operating in daily life through an individual personality.

How to transcend the negative ego

In this section I will explore popular and traditional methods for transcending the negative ego. It must be noted however that these practices best suit ascension seekers at the Indigo and Crystal levels of consciousness. However at the Rainbow and Diamond levels of consciousness transcendence of the negative ego comes about when the light of the Universal Awareness dissolves the identification that we have with ego and personality. I will write about this in the section called Advanced Ascension. At these levels Ascension is not about doing anything but being a different way completely.

Self Enquiry

A common method is the practice of Self-Enquiry. This is the process of consistently monitoring our own personal thoughts and feelings. It is a skill that can be developed so that we become a witness to our thoughts and emotions. It is a well known spiritual practice that has been taught by such individuals such as Sai Baba and other leading saints and gurus throughout the ages. The practice of then replacing negative thoughts with positive thoughts is at the core of this process. It is also the basis of cognitive therapies made popular in recent years in the western world. Within these therapies there is the realisation that positive thoughts can influence the experience of positive emotions. In truth everyone should follow this practice as it greatly enhances the experience of life and helps us to be more joyful, balanced and aware of our spirituality. The difficulty does not lie in understanding the process of self enquiry but rather the in the ability to skilfully apply the process in everyday life. The process proves to be too problematic for most people and hence this chapter offers insights and solutions to these challenges.

There is also the reality that our actual awareness of our negative ego in the moments when this arises is sometimes enough to dismantle the negative ego at that point and in those circumstances. It is therefore possible to grow your own awareness of the negative ego as a tool for transcending it. This must all be done without a sense of personal criticism or judgement.

Why is self enquiry necessary? The process of ascension includes transcending the negative ego. This includes the replacement of negative thoughts and feelings with positive ones as we monitor the operation of our ego. The only way we can be aware of when we are having negative thoughts and feelings is if we are on the lookout for them. Most people are simply not aware of their own thoughts and feelings and how these are creating their personal reality. They react to situations and usually express their lower self through anger or fear. Instead we can respond to situations in a controlled and spiritual way. Again it is not commonly known that our thoughts directly influence our emotions. It is always good to remember that ascension work is not about being good in the eyes of God, the ascended masters or whoever. It is all about removing us from pain, suffering and isolation. Nobody enjoys negative experiences.

Only we can think our personal thoughts or feel our emotions. This is our responsibility alone. As such if we allow ourselves to operate in these negative ways then it will be us who suffer the consequences. No amounts of prayers are going to undo the effect of our unwitting creating undesirable situations through our own negativity. The desire to no longer suffer at the hands of the negative ego should be enough of a motivation to encourage us to practice self enquiry every day. Some people feel that their suffering and negativity is normal and unavoidable. This is an illusion created by the negative ego thinking. Every person has the ability to change and transform their lives through such techniques as self enquiry.

Another motivation is the desire to enjoy those things that we need and want in life. These could be such things as additional financial abundance, a romantic relationship or the opportunity to grow or serve in spiritual ways. The ability to deliberately attract to us these opportunities, people and situations is called the manifestation process. It is the universal law that our thoughts and feelings attract people and events that are a match in vibration or quality. As such in truth everyone is already manifesting many things in their lives through their thoughts and emotions. They do not recognise this as the results are often negative reflecting the negative content of these thoughts and emotions. When we make the deliberate choice to replace negative thoughts and feelings with positive one we begin the process of manifesting what we actually want rather than what we do not want. We do not want negative thoughts and feelings attracting undesirable experiences into our lives. And so we can agree that we all need a method of preventing this. Self enquiry is again to tool that we use to achieve this. By this method we recognise negative and therefore harmful thoughts and emotions and we can then take steps to stop them.

Becoming Aware of negative thoughts and feelings

Here are three areas in which we can all notice the underlying presence of negative thoughts:

Within our casual thoughts – If you monitor your thoughts you will occasionally catch individual and random thoughts. You may be surprised that you have thought such things. These thoughts often give clues to the underlying belief system.

Within our conversations – When we talk to other people we sometimes express deep beliefs and emotions that we were not aware of ourselves at a conscious level. If you have a close friend or family member then they often act as a type of counsellor and in our discussions much can be revealed. Instead of just getting things off our chest, we can pay attention to what we are saying and feeling as these are golden clues.

Within our emotions – Our emotions can ALWAYS reveal our true relationship to a person, situation or idea. If we train ourselves to acknowledge them and become more aware of our emotions then they will reveal the general content of our thoughts and belief systems. You can ask yourself "what do I feel about this person / situation?" If there are feelings such as doubt, fear, or anger then it is highly likely there are negative thoughts and belief systems in operation. Other people or situations do not cause these emotions as they represent our current experience of our own thoughts. We must not blame other people for our own perceptions and experiences. This is called projection and is a denial of the true cause of our experience. Instead we take responsibility for our own thoughts and transform them so that our experience changes in positive ways. Positive emotions may reveal the presence of positive thoughts and belief systems. Good examples of positive emotions are joy, hope, excitement and the senses of ease, freedom and empowerment.

Self Enquiry in Action

Where we find negative thought patterns we can implement attitudinal healing. This is where we consider the existing thoughts and find higher ways of looking at the subject. We can then adopt the higher way of looking at the subject and make this our new approach or response. Here are some examples:

Example 1

Situation: Someone has been rude to us!

Common negative ego reaction: to be angry, to want revenge for hurt feelings.

Higher response: to detach from the incident and to not take offence. To possibly recognise the other person's problems which are being expressed in their negative behaviour. To choose to forgive them and to desire a healing outcome for the situation.

Insight: Society teaches us that in this situation we are justified in being angry. The problem is that if we agree with this then we are locking ourselves into a cycle of negative thoughts and feelings which are not enjoyable and affect our energies and experience of life. This approach could even program more undesirable thoughts into our sub-conscious mind such as:

"I am a weak person and people will always pick on me"

"Everyone is rude to me!"

"I hate people!"

"I need to be more defensive as people are attacking me!"

These potential thoughts can become programmed into the sub-conscious mind. These add to previous similar negative thoughts from the past and form patterns. These patterns form the foundation of what we think is reality and we then begin to attract similar situations into our lives through the manifestation process. This can become a cycle of negativity until we end it by choosing higher ways to look at this situation and start to re-program our sub-conscious mind.

Example 2

Situation: We appear to be failing in attracting to us service work opportunities, financial abundance or desirable relationships.

Common negative ego reaction: To be angry with other people and ultimately to be angry with God. To then fall into despair and to indulge in negative and self destructive thoughts about self such as "I am not good enough." "Nobody loves me." "I do not deserve to have the things that I want." " I will never get what I want."

Higher self response: To understand that there are divine reasons for all situations and ultimately these serve us. To want to understand these divine reasons, plans and timings. To want to complete any learning that is a part of this. To want to take responsibility for manifesting what is required and desired in the most skilful way. To no longer look to others for what we want but to co-create with the divine opportunities that best serves our needs.

Resisting the Negative Ego

The wonderful benefit of using self-enquiry consistently is that it allows us to witness our own patterns of thoughts, emotion and behaviour. This brings insight and helps us to be clear about our own ascension work requirements. We soon learn about our own issues and areas that need our attention. These will inevitably be different from other people as the ascension journey is different for all of us. We know what "pushes our buttons" and where we are most likely to succumb to lower self thinking and behaviour. We may find that we understand intellectually that we want to experience higher ways of thinking and behaviour and yet sometimes we do not achieve this. Why? The negative ego provides us with a sense of satisfaction when it convinces us that the fear based thoughts were justified. We find it hard to shake off these patterns of thought and behaviour even when we understand intellectually that this is the right thing to do. Our aim with self-enquiry is to perfect it to the degree that it is running almost in real time capacity. Here we are witnessing our thoughts and emotions seconds after they are expressed. This can be achieved simply through practice and discipline. This level of self-enquiry allows us to RESIST falling into these old patterns of negative thought and behaviour. We can see them coming and we can deny them. Our desire to experience a higher way of being becomes stronger than the attraction to that which the negative ego offers in terms of being right or in control. We choose love, compassion and harmony instead of being right, better and separate from others. We cannot have both and so we need to choose one. In truth we may not achieve this aim a lot of the time. However in time we find it easier and find that we are expressing our higher will more and more. This is the experience of transcending the negative ego. Daily life is our guide and teacher. We attract people and situations that allow us the opportunities to practice making these choices. These are commonly called spiritual lessons and may involve friends, family and work colleagues. When we have perfected any specific lesson then we find that we no longer attract those particular situations into our daily life as we move onto new areas of learning and practice. Key points are:

We need to resist old negative patterns and choose to experience higher ones

It is not enough to intellectually understand how to transcend the negative ego. We need to actually demonstrate this in daily life

This process takes a lot of discipline as it needs to be consistent. Without this progress stops

Advanced Self- Enquiry

In the early days, self-enquiry may be a general practice. Over time you will become aware of the recurring themes that affect you personally the most as you will have noticed them. The same techniques can be used for these specific themes. Let us say that you have noticed that the theme of forgiveness keep coming up in life's challenges and your experiences. Here you can be on alert to work with this theme for a while until you have made progress with it. It is possible to have several specific focuses at any one time and indeed there will always be opportunities to work on some aspect of self. You can make it your priority to make progress with these themes and this becomes a pro-active approach. Indeed these pro-active approaches save us a lot of difficulty as they are working with problems and potential problems before they become very big issues in our spiritual process. Earth is a school of learning where traditionally the motivation to grow and transform is provided as a result of the experiences of pain and suffering. The typical human experience is to maintain the "status quo" until something comes along that persuades us differently. This is often a challenge in life which highlights some part of self that needs attention such as negative emotions. We often resist these challenges until the motivation to transform is greater than the will to resist growth. This is a typical lower consciousness approach. A higher way of being is to learn through grace. This is to be open to learning through divine wisdom and love. Here we learn to willingly embrace change and transformation without resisting it. This removes the experience of great challenge and suffering as there is no resistance. We grow gracefully with ease. To work with grace we have to be very skilled at the art of self-enquiry and benefit from the deep awareness of self that this brings. Here we can respond quickly to ever-changing patterns of growth, working with these in whatever ways we need to in the moment. We can listen to the whisperings of our souls and guides and address growth patterns in the moment rather than later on when they have become more problematic. We can seek guidance from the Universe and we can be sincerely open to embracing this. This provides a flowing experience where we grow quickly and more easily. Indeed we can be very pro-active with our growth agendas by looking ahead and preparing for these. For example for those within the Ascension movement there are two major areas of expansion that will certainly be experienced. These are:

The movement towards oneness and inclusiveness within humanity

At the later stages of ascension, the transcendence of the human identity / personality and earthly desires

We can work on these now by considering our thoughts and emotions regarding these coming experiences and advanced levels of consciousness. This is self enquiry working in advance and all the same techniques can be used to prepare us and remove any negative and limiting aspects. This is a powerful and wise way to work.

Surrender

The spiritual path is one of transformation and change becomes the core theme. The level of change required with the Ascension process is demanding as it is the transformation of consciousness itself. This inevitably influences change within all parts of our life such as:

our thoughts, belief systems,
values, morality, ethics
emotions, moods
energy fields, the energetic flow to our chakras, presence of energetic blocks
our behaviour, how we spend our free time, our activities, our relationships
our occupations
our spiritual abilities, ability to meditate,
spiritual qualities such as wisdom, compassion, unconditional love

Many people exercise poor choices in relationships, occupations and personal behaviour. Often they are aware of this and yet there seems a resistance to change these situations that is illogical and without apparent reason. It seems as if something is better than nothing. There is a tendency for all of us to hold onto that which is familiar even when it really does not serve us. Humanity loves that which is familiar. These things give us a sense of identity and so we seek to preserve them. Who would we be without such things? Of course these tendencies are challenged in the ascension process and in spiritual growth in general. This is why there are not so many volunteers to embark on the journey of ascension! However for those who are ascension seekers then your relationship to change and transformation will be the theme of your life. Transformation is not merely accepting the principle of change on an intellectual level. It is the active and willing participation in the process of change at every level of our being. This includes intellectually, emotionally, spiritually and energetically. It has to be this way as you cannot have change and resistance to change existing side by side. As such we must be comfortable with letting go of old thoughts, feelings and energies. When we do this voluntarily so that we can experience higher ways of being, *we surrender.*

My full definition of surrender is *"**to let go of resistance to personal change and transformation"**.*

It is our own resistance to change and transformation that is the real issue here. Our relationship to our resistance defines our reality and how we experience it. Do we embrace growth and change or do we resist it? Do you learn through grace or through pain? Resistance to change causes pain and discomfort. A lack of resistance allows an experience of ease, flow and grace to our process. We take steps to grow and learn and yet all the time we have our foot hovering over the brake in case the actual experience is not what we imagined or wanted! And so surrendering is taking our foot away from the brake and implementing a positive movement towards accepting, allowing and embracing the process even if it is not what we imagined.

The word surrender has negative connotations implying that we are giving in to someone else's will. Other connotations include dishonour, failure and a loss of control. I suggest we substitute the word *remember* for surrender. The soul holds the knowledge of why we came to earth and what ideally we would accomplish here as a life mission. As such surrender involves remembering what this is and aligning our thoughts and activities to this. This may involve changing aspects of our life, however this is what we have planned for ourselves before we came into this incarnation.

At the personality level another reason for resistance to surrender is because at a deep level we know that surrender involves facing our "demons". These are old pains, traumas, negative experiences that we have blocked out of our every day awareness but still exist in our sub-conscious mind and energy bodies. There may be emotions and belief systems that have been carried over from previous lifetimes.

We feel fear and apprehension when we start to do this. The reason that these unresolved parts of self need to be healed and cleared is so we can embrace the highest level of consciousness that we can maintain. This can only be achieved if we transcend fear which involves acknowledging, healing and clearing these un-resolved parts of self. In reality the fear of fear and pain is usually much worse than the act of healing ourselves. It is unquestionably better for us to tackle these outstanding issues even if they bring some discomfort as we approach them.

Resistance requires a tremendous amount of energy to maintain. Resistance = tiredness and depression. With full and unconditionally surrender we experience a huge sense of relief from this. We feel lighter, peaceful and more energised. The natural state of being is to be connected the divine and expressing our life missions. This is what God and our souls always intended for us. When we recognise this and remember / surrender then we allow the joy and deep contentment that this natural state brings to be in our life.

Within the ascension process there is a continual need to surrender different aspects of self at different stages. Each phase of ascension requires a new and different type of surrender

Additional Techniques for transcending the negative ego

Affirmations - Affirmations are commonly used to assist with attitudinal healing. These are positive statements that are expressed often. These can be general or tailor made by us to serve our focus at that time. Examples of affirmations are:

"I am able to forgive everyone in my life!"

"I am financially abundant now!"

"I am loveable and I love myself!"

Affirmations help to program the sub-conscious mind with positive belief systems. This in turn will help to transform our emotions in positive ways. I would recommend that specific affirmations are repeated for a period of forty days and used about three times a day. To make the affirmations super effective, we can spend a moment feeling the emotions NOW that would be present when the content of the affirmation is actually present in our life. This will change our energies so that we are more likely to attract to us these new people, situations and opportunities that we desire. This is the key factor of all manifestation work.

Visualisations - We can visualise anything we like through the imagination. This is the ability to see things or "imagine" them in our mind rather than seeing them in the physical world around us. This is a type of viewing screen that can used to project onto it the reflections of our thoughts and our experiences in other dimensions of reality. This is a powerful exercise in creating positive thoughts that help re-program the sub-conscious mind and help to encourage the positive flow of energies and general well being.

An example of a visualisation are images of you sitting or walking around enjoying whatever quality it is that you are aiming to attract into your experience. Alternatively it could be you enjoying the freedom from any negative qualities that you are currently experiencing. Once again in order to make the affirmations super effective, we can spend a moment feeling the emotions NOW that would be present when the content of the affirmation is actually present in our life.

When I use the word "imagine" I am not using the connotation that the image you see if unreal but instead that it is an image that is part of the real and creative part of the mind. When you visualise things in your imagination or onto your viewing screen what you see is a reflection of the creation of your thoughts. For example If you visualise or imagine that a bubble of white light surrounds you then this thought WILL attract this event to you. Please have complete faith and trust that your visualisations will have an effect with or without any confirmation experienced by you.

Some people are not very visual and so trying to visualise things may be difficult. In this case working with pure intentions is very effective. Here we simply make it our intention to think and feel a certain way. It is an inner commitment that influences how we approach people and events. If we are consistent with setting our intentions then we can positively influence our energies and how we experience our reality. The more power and focus we put into our intentions then the more impact they will have. In our example our person may simply make it their intention to be open to forgiving their parents in all opportunities. This helps to liberate them from past patterns of negative thought and emotion and encourages new and positive experiences to be had.

Humility & Humour

The negative ego promotes attitudes of anger, pride and arrogance. Even when these appear justifiable in certain situations, to express these is to allow the negative ego to perpetuate illusions and negativity. Humility is a great tool for disarming the negative ego. Self importance, pride and arrogance are all expressions of fear and separateness thinking. They bring a sense of satisfaction that needs to be denied. By practising humility we disarm the negative ego expression. When we move deeply into spiritual awareness it is not hard to be humble when we experience the wonder of life and God. When we are distracted from this wonder we allow opportunities for the negative ego to become alive. As such it is always good to allow and develop humility and humour in a balanced way. Humility when unbalanced can lead to a lack of will and confidence and the inability to manifest. Humour too disarms the negative ego. By this I mean the genuine humorous attitudes where the subject of the humour is not victimised.

Who Am I? Identification

When we identify with something we are aware of it, we give it importance and we make it "real". Whatever we identify with creates our reality and our place in that reality. Who we are is then defined by our relationship to that which we are aware of in our own reality. We interact with those things we identify with and they give us our sense of self. If we do not identify with something then it is because we are either not aware of it or we do not give it importance and therefore it does not enter into our reality. It is important to acknowledge that we all do this and that the process of identification is at the heart of spiritual growth and ascension. What we identify with has a direct correlation with our level of spiritual growth and ascension. More specifically the level of our personal spiritual growth and ascension is most directly influences by those aspects of our self that we identify with as being most important to us. Here I mean such aspects as our thoughts (conscious and sub conscious), emotions, energies, inner senses, soul and spirit (universal awareness). When we switch our identification of self (who we think, feel and sense that we are) from one level to a higher level then we expand our consciousness and we grow spiritually.

The process of ascension is ultimately about what you identify with at any one time. If we identify with our ego and personality then we operate from lower consciousness. If we identify with our soul and spirit then we allow these aspects to work through the personality and ego and express themselves on earth. This is higher consciousness. However it is what you identify with which will either make the process easy or hard. If you still identify with personality and ego (your past, pain and limitation) then you will resist the natural process of ascension. If you let go of your identification of your ego and personality then you will embrace the natural process of ascension which is to return to the higher consciousness of the soul and spirit in a graceful way. This process feels like a series of mini deaths and it is. It is the death of your identification with your ego. At times it feels as if something has been taken away, but you will notice the higher consciousness that has replaced it and this is much more satisfying as it brings hope, joy and freedom. This process will continue in phases.

Identification as experienced within the different levels of human consciousness

A lower consciousness person mainly identifies with the material world and the physical senses. At this level a typical person not engaged in spiritual practice or psychological exploration. There is often little awareness of the different aspects of self such as soul and spirit. They are not even aware of many of their own thoughts or emotions. In their reality life is really just a series of reactions to seemingly outside events happening to "me". Often this leads to the identification with the role of the victim. In this state they are mainly unconscious and run on auto pilot. The expressions of their negative ego and personality dominate their experiences and as such much negativity is experienced in their reality. There is little awareness of any spiritual realities.

After a spiritual awakening some enter into the Indigo level of consciousness. An awakened spiritual seeker (Indigo) identifies with their thoughts and their emotional responses to the world around them. They are seeking deeper understandings to their spiritual and philosophical questions. Here less importance is placed on the physical and materialistic worlds. Identification is now switching from the physical world outside of self to the inner worlds of thought and emotion. "I" becomes not just a physical being but also a being with a spiritual component mainly experienced through the intellect but also through emotions and occasional mystical experiences. In relation to the world around us, "I" appears to be an individual but with a growing sense of a mystical connection to the world and universe that is yet to be defined or fully experienced.

A Crystal level being identifies with the unseen worlds and dimensions of spiritual energies and realities as perceived through their inner senses and revealed by their soul. Here less importance is placed on the intellectual experience of spirituality. Identification is now switching from the intellectual to experiences of connection to people and the world at large. This is brought about by through a soul infused emotional reconnection to life experienced as a pure and expanding love of all things. "I" becomes not just a physical being experiencing spirituality through the intellect, but also a being remembering a universal love that is the essence of the soul and remembering how this allows the experience of oneness. In relation to the world around us, "I" appears to be an individual but this identity becomes more blurred as "I" is also exists as universal love which also brings the realisation of a way being and belonging that is outside of the body, thoughts and personality. Universal love here is still focused mainly in the physical world with a sense of kinship with people, acknowledgement of the loving support of the divine in their life as well as an appreciation of magnificence of all forms of nature.

A Rainbow level being identifies with multi dimensional realities including spirit (universal awareness). Identification is now switching from the intellectual and the exploration of universal love in the outer world to the inner worlds of mystical experiences, intuition and contemplation (a receptive state of being allowing communication with the divine that leads to illumination, inspiration and revelation). "I" becomes not just a physical, intellectual and loving being, but also a being with a growing awareness of their own connection to unseen dimensions of spiritual realities. In relation to the world around us, "I" appears to be an individual but also exists elsewhere in other dimensions. As such "I" is not longer defined as just being "here" in the physical world but also being "there" in other dimensions. This is a profound change in identification.

A Diamond level being identifies with spirit and the expression of spirit in this world. They are not just exploring their connections to universal awareness but they are also expressing spirit in the world through their presence. "I" is not just a multi dimensional being aware of its condition in a somewhat passive way, but becomes consciously active in aligning itself with universal awareness and finding ways to channel this in the physical world.

Death of the Ego

As such Ascension is all about the process of continually changing what we identify with. This transforms us greatly. Another way of describing ascension is that it is a process of allowing our identity to die in order that a greater identity can emerge. In ancient Egypt spiritual growth was referred to a series of mini deaths. Indeed for those who experience a profound change in identity and ascend to another level, there are these feelings associated with death. Here I mean the feelings of a loss of something very intimate and a sense of having to come to terms with something new and unfamiliar. This can be a grieving experience that leads to the process of identification with a new expanded level of consciousness. These are the experiences of people in the ascension process. However the Golden Ascension mantra that I use applies here more than anywhere else. ***"We only have two choices, to resist change or to embrace change!"*** Clearly those who embrace change have a more gentle and graceful experience of ascension. We can look at this in detail later on in the book.

Physical death itself is a type of ascension. If you believe in the afterlife then you may be familiar with how those who have experienced physical death also experience undergoing a transformation in personal consciousness. This is reported by those who have near death experiences and from those who communicate from the afterlife through mediums. A person of lower consciousness will mainly identify with their physical body as being who they are and the physical world as being their reality. When they physically die these things are taken away from them. They have to profoundly change their identification of self as they find their awareness in new reality and hence their consciousness expands. However ascension for many means going through this process whilst still being physically alive. My book describes the ascension process in detail explaining how we change our identification and personal realities along the way. It is the journey of how our identification with the physical world as our reality gradually switches to the unseen spiritual realities and then ultimately to the reality of spirit or universal awareness.

Ascension Integration

The Ascension process involves the raising of consciousness from one distinct level to another. Within this expansion there are profound changes in our aura and energetic bodies. Our energy fields expand and merge with larger energetic fields. We become more than before. These changes also influence our personality, thoughts and emotions. We literally become a different type of person. Within all of this change it takes time to integrate the changes so that which was new becomes normal. This process can be intense and challenging as so this chapter explores the nature of integration and we can assist this process.

What are the common problems after a period of spiritual transformation?

Often there is physical tiredness and lethargy. Our emotions include apathy, feelings of loss, and the desire to enjoy that which brings familiarity. Mentally we experience confusion and the inability to focus.

Understanding the Process of Ascension as we rise from one level to another:

Activation
↓
Resistance
↓
Negotiation
↓
Surrender
↓
Acclimatisation

Activation:

As already written, it is often the simple and well established spiritual activities that are the most effective in activating spiritual growth. If individuals regularly practice these then progress can be made with activating ascension. This is an interactive process with the Universe and we attract opportunities to transform our consciousness. Daily life becomes our practice ground for the new spiritual agendas we explore. Within this our spiritual lessons persist until we fully integrate and embody the current learning.

Self enquiry – To choose higher thoughts and emotions. To transcend the negative ego

Prayer – to seek assistance from the universe, to become clear about your requirements

Contemplation – to think and wonder about the deepest nature of your spiritual existence, to be open to receiving new insights and experiences

Meditation – to expand consciousness, to quieten the mind and become aware of your divine presence, to allow communication from guides, angels, intuition etc

Divine Connection - To seek Divine experiences. This includes anything that lifts your consciousness such as nature, art, music etc.

Resistance / Denial

At a conscious level we are often not aware of what growth patterns exist within the ascension phase that we are in. However we are a complex system and within us is awareness of what needs to be surrendered, healed and transcended.

Messages are sent to our personality by these aspects. The content of the messages is often uncomfortable to us as it involves dealing with our repressed negative emotions or negative thought patterns that we have held for many years or many lifetimes. These messages may reach us through our dreams or through an emerging awareness in daily life.

Initially we may try to deny this process so that our personality can remain "protected" from these painful aspects. The negative ego will certainly try and block these messages as they threaten its survival and ultimately they will remove its powerful weapon of survival which is fear. However these messages are really only instructions about how to release these negative aspects. They come as part of the ascension plan and come in response to our efforts towards spiritual growth.

Our resistance to the ascension messages and instructions can create friction within us which is experienced in different ways. These are the outer expressions reflecting the inner resistance and turmoil that is taking place. There can be general anxiety as well as heightened negative thoughts and emotions. Sleep can become disturbed causing nightmares, insomnia and bed sweats. There can be physical ailments such as skin problems and headaches. Fatigue, lethargy and mild depression can result. Spiritually we feel disconnected, as there is great turmoil within us which distracts us from our spiritual connections. Often the personality is still unaware of the reasons behind these experiences. Life becomes challenging and some seek to blame others for their difficult experiences in an attempt to find meaning in this chaos.

Supportive Strategies

Find the source of resistance and work on this by going inwards within your prayers, meditations and following your intuition.

Look at your emotions. Understand what is causing negative emotions. Are there any old repeating patterns? What challenges are you attracting to yourself in life? Your emotions are your clues as they reflect your inner worlds and realities.

Negotiation

At some point our personality may become partially aware of these resistance patterns and the inner work which is required. We may then seek positive change within our life in an attempt to assist these processes.

Often the "price" of change appears too high and we seek compromises and the justifications for doing these. These compromises rarely work and yet this becomes a strategy that allows us to feel more comfortable about the process and prepares us to eventually complete the inner work. We realise that a partial surrender does not work and that we are required to fully complete this area of inner work and experience. It is unavoidable. When this happens we give up resistance to the process and allow surrender.

Supportive Strategies

Trust that letting go of resistance is the best thing that you can do, even if you do not know where it is leading you!

This is the time to be the spiritual warrior and to find our inner strength which is needed to complete this process and let go of the old. This is the real work of transformation.

Find that which connects to you spirit / God such as the being in nature or through art and music. This brings us a reminder of the beauty and magnificence of the Universe around us. This makes it easier to surrender to our spiritual path when we feel connected to the power and perfection of a benign Universe which will support us in our task.

Surrender

Surrender happens when we fundamentally change our approach to our current growth experience. We need to really want the higher way of being offered more than the familiarity of old ways or to avoid any discomfort from the process. We go from resistance to allowing.

True surrender happens when we realise the lessons and growth patterns at deep levels and not just in understanding them intellectually. Sometimes we do not understand the process intellectually as surrender comes from the centre of our being and not from our mind. It can happen in a moment of profound realisation or it can take some time. It feels like a huge release as resisting things takes a lot of energy and causes negative experiences. We feel light, free and positive.

Sometimes just prior to surrender we can experience intense physical release in the letting go of resistance. There can be fevers, vomiting and diarrhoea. This is especially true in the earlier phases of ascension where there is more resistance and negativity to overcome.

At other times and especially in later levels of ascension, surrender becomes an ecstatic release and we experience brief moments of profound and blissful oneness with the Universe. It is at these times that we are blessed with glimpses of how it is to ascend and merge in energy, consciousness and purpose with the Universe.

As we experience different ascension phases we learn that the experience of these processes is in our own hands. It is our choice as to how much we resist or how quickly we align our efforts to the ascension process and surrender at each stage. It is possible to have a graceful experience of ascension. As we master ourselves we also become a master of the ascension process itself. We can be aware at every stage what we are experiencing and what is needed to assist. We seek balance, integration and an allowing approach at all times.

Supportive Strategies

Often in the process of surrender we seek isolation, retreats and private ceremonies. This allows us the space to go inwards and confront our resistance and then allow surrender. In that process the Universe draws close to us and it supports us and it sends confirmation to us which is received in a myriad of ways. This is a time for trust and courage

Other supportive strategies include removing internal resistance to change and transformation. Our resistance is our choice and can be removed by letting it go.

Here we make it our intention to let go of what is needed to be let go of. Emotionally we let go of fearful and negative emotions holding us back. Intellectually we accept that we do not have to understand the issues or process fully before we can let go of something. We can understand that this process is necessary and that it will benefit us. Physically we can relax and let go of tension through deep breathing exercises. Rest and sleep are more important now than normal.

Acclimatisation

At the end of a stage we feel different as we have changed and moved into a higher level of being. We experience a type of grieving process. This is a **mini death** of an old part of ourselves that we have known for many years. We are grieving the loss of familiarity of the old self. This can last for days and weeks. As humans we crave familiarity more than we realise.

When we move into a higher level of being our sense of self becomes new and unfamiliar. Our natural reactions are to cling to that which is familiar. We may cling to old habits as if nothing has happened. Ultimately we come to accept the new higher level of self. And so there forms a period when we temporarily deny the new energies and level of being and search for anything that reminds us of our old self. Ultimately we come to terms with the death of the old self and accept the new higher way. At this point we begin to enjoy our higher energies. We feel elated, joyful and free. We notice and enjoy the higher aspects of our being. We may feel higher emotions such as unconditional love, peace or compassion. We sense the absence of the influence of the negative ego more than before. This results in less fear being present in all aspects of life. We notice that we become more non-attached to other people's negativity. We notice that it is easier to have more positive thoughts. For those who are sensitive to their auras, they may feel that their energies are different reflecting this ascension growth. Within a short period of time we become adjusted to this higher level. Life becomes easier for a while as we simple exist at this level until we approach the next ascension "spurt". It becomes hard to remember the previous version of self. Where many mini ascension "spurts" have taken place then it may be that a person becomes unrecognisable in many ways to others and even to themselves such are the change that take place to the personality.

At some stage during the ascension "spurt", the operation of our energetic bodies and chakras changes. This is in response to the changes in our consciousness and the progress within the ascension process. We may become more aware of higher dimensions and the flow of higher spiritual energies through our systems. We may notice our expanded energy fields and the greater multi-dimensional awareness that we have. At the point where this is first noticed it can be experienced as a blissful feeling. It is truly a spiritual revelation and can very enjoyable. There are feelings of being "plugged in" to expanded awareness. It is sensual and loving. There can also be the feelings of being dizzy and ungrounded. Thinking can become difficult and physical exercise more tiring than normal. General tiredness is common. This period can last for hours or for days. It is part of the acclimatisation process.

<u>Supportive Strategies</u>

Rest during tired phases. Be kind to yourself by letting go of obligations and put your own needs first for a while.

Physically we need additional water and grounding food. Grounding food helps us to reconnect to our body and the physical realms and is often rich in proteins and fat. Some find coffee especially grounding.

Being rather than doing! This is how higher consciousness is! This includes resting, contemplating, day dreaming, being quiet and reflective. By giving yourself time and space to be aware of your own raised consciousness you will integrate the new energies and the notice the differences. If you throw yourself into the usual busy activities of daily life then you probably not notice any changes and lose this opportunity.

Resist going back to old negative habits, thoughts and emotions. They will only bring you discomfort.

Advanced Ascension ways of being

At the higher levels of Ascension our approaches to spiritual growth change. We need different spiritual activities that reflect the realities of the higher consciousness that we find ourselves experiencing. The rules have changed and so must we. Here are some of the most powerful insights and approaches that we can use with Ascension and they are especially relevant to those experiencing Rainbow and Diamond Levels of consciousness. First of all we must embrace Universal Awareness which is how we experience the higher levels of Ascension and which I will explain later. The route to this involves appreciating that our thoughts and emotions are not what we previously imagined them to be. We must lose our identification with our thoughts and emotions and embrace the higher perceptions of Universal Awareness.

Thoughts

If I was to ask you, "where do *you* exist in your body?" Most people would identify with the idea that they exist in their heads or brains from where it is believed that thoughts operate from. The activity of thinking and the content of these thoughts are considered by many to be the essence of who they are. However it is vital to understand that in essence we are not our thoughts. The greatest spiritual truth is that we are awareness itself and yet we do not recognise this often as this awareness is dominated by our thoughts and daily activities. Those who allow their awareness to expand beyond their thoughts discover that they are able to become aware of awareness itself. This leads to enlightenment and freedom from the restrictions of lower consciousness. Therefore the popular expression "I think therefore I am" is misleading. It should be stated "I am awareness therefore I am!"

It is within meditation that we become aware of our awareness itself. We experience it as simply existing (being). In the normal function of thinking we are merely aware of the content of our thoughts. We can choose not to engage with our thoughts within meditation. With some practice we can learn how not to allow our awareness to be sucked into the thoughts patterns. When we do this we start to quieten the mind and end the distractions of thinking. We can then allow our awareness simply to be. Here there is peace and tranquillity and within that awareness emerges insights, knowing and realisations which are more expansive experiences than with pure thinking. In time we identify with our awareness and not with our thoughts. We might answer my original question differently then. Instead of existing in the head we might feel that we also exist outside of our body within pure consciousness wherever you might imagine that may be. Why is this important? It is because the higher consciousness of ascension is found when pure awareness is allowed to expand and when we no longer allow it to be dominated by thinking. As such the sooner an ascension seeker avoids the trap of over identifying with and overindulging with thinking then the sooner they will allow themselves opportunities to become aware of awareness itself and then to explore this further.

Thinking vs. knowing

The human mind thinks. This is the process of collecting information and experiences which the mind processes and analyses. Our mind presents to our awareness temporary conclusions or beliefs based on its analysis. However the mind never stops this process and so it is always in search of new information and experiences. It is never satisfied. As such the mind never knows anything for certain as its conclusions are always subject to change. With thinking therefore there are always doubts. When people explore spirituality through the mind alone there is always frustration that comes about because this pure thinking leads to doubts. What people really want is to know things for certain and better still to actually have a personal experience of them.

When we know something there is no doubt about it. What is the colour of your house or car? You simply know the answer to these questions. There is no need to think about it or analyse it. It is what it is. There is no thinking taking place. Imagine knowing the answer to a lot of things and especially about spiritual realities. This is how the Universal Awareness speaks to us in clear, calm and deep ways. It allows us to know without having to think. We have realisations where we know something at a deep enough level that it is felt at every level of our being.

The human mind was never made to understand the deepest secrets of the Universe by thinking alone. The problem comes about when people try to experience spirituality through the mind alone. They try and intellectualise spirituality and ultimately this limits their experience it. What is needed is the ability to move beyond the mind into pure knowing and intuition which comes about when we communicate directly with the universe using our inner senses.

Emotions

Our emotions are actually a feedback system that tells us what we are experiencing in our personal reality. If you actually examine your emotions, you will notice that they are temporary experiences perhaps lasting for seconds or minutes. Ideally emotions should flow and be felt with new emotions coming all of the time. The type of emotion you experience in the moment reflects back to you what is happening at deep levels within your entire being in that precise moment. Nobody can make us feel specific emotions. Instead what we feel is influenced by how we react and respond to what is happening in our outer and inner world experiences. If you are aware of this you can monitor your emotions to find out what is going in your reality. This is useful as we have sub conscious thoughts patterns and we are not always consciously aware of the content of these. Through our emotions we can get clues to the existence and the content of certain sub conscious mind thought patterns.

For most people emotions become blocked and repressed. This leads to an ongoing negative pattern of resistance to feeling these emotions and this leads to suffering. Sadly such people reach the conclusion that this dysfunctional pattern is normal and that all emotions are negative.

The interaction between Thoughts and Emotion

It is universally understood that our thoughts influence our emotions. It is the basis of cognitive therapy as well as much spiritual psychological work. Where we have negative thoughts then these lead to negative emotions such as anger, jealously and despair. Where we have positive thoughts we can experience positive emotions such as happiness, satisfaction, love and excitement.

However this is only part of the true understanding of the inter relationship between thoughts and emotions. There are those experiences which cannot strictly be called emotions. These result from the workings of the inner senses which give us a more expansive experience. These include the senses of well being, meaning, bliss and ecstasy. They enter into our experiences not as the result of a thought but as a reflection of our chosen reality. Our reality is our map of all creation in which we include or exclude spiritual dimensions. That which we call real or true becomes our reality. In a deeper sense that which we resist falls outside of our reality and that which we embrace becomes our reality. Evolved spiritual seekers entertain a large reality and as a result they regularly experience these inner senses which act as a feedback system. They tell us how near we are to God or how far away we are. A lack of experience of these inner senses comes about when we are too focused in the physical world and then spiritual dimensions start to fade and move outside of our reality. Inner sense experiences tell us that we are very spiritually aligned to spiritual dimensions and that the universe / God are actively responding to our choices to expand our reality. God seeks to reveal itself at all levels and so when we start invite this process into our life then a response is received. God is interactive!

Inner senses

As we evolve we increasingly perceive things through our inner senses (see language of the universal consciousness). These inner senses give us a deeper understanding and experience of all things than the physical senses can. One such sense is the ability to be sensitive to spiritual energies. There is a dimension where spiritual energies exist for all things and these energies describe the quality and nature of everything. As we read these energies we gain access to deep insights that are pure and truthful. Within higher consciousness there is a gradual switch from a thinking and emotional relationship to what we encounter in spiritual terms to one which "reads" the spiritual energies of people, places and situations.

Universal Awareness

Universal Awareness has also been called our spirit, "beingness" or the "I am" presence. I call it the Universal Awareness with great reason. This name correctly implies that it is connected to the Universe or all that is. In the evolved and later stages of human spiritual consciousness this becomes the major theme to explore. Unlike our physical bodies, our Universal Awareness is not limited by its construction nor is it separate from other beings. My Universal Awareness can merge with the Universal Awareness of you or any number of people. It is nonphysical after all and so is not subject to the limitations in the physical world. Perhaps it is more accurate to say that we can remember that we are already merged within the Universal Awareness and we can allow that reality into our consciousness. The common motivation at higher levels of consciousness is to continually experience more expanded states of consciousness through merging with expanded energy fields. Ultimately the merged energy fields and consciousness of all beings is God or source. When we identify with our Universal Awareness as being "me" or "I" more than our thoughts, then we have transcended normal human consciousness and we have become the enlightened mystical traveller. It is not an exaggeration to say, that this very realisation is possibly the most important of all. It changes everything.

However the majority of people are so distracted by their thoughts and emotions that they fail to be aware of their own awareness. It is particularly a problem in the west where the intellect is valued more than the spirit and where life is often lived at such a quick pace that time is not allocated to being peaceful and reflective. This is why traditional meditation is recognised as a powerful tool in spiritual growth. Traditional Meditation is a technique to explore what happens when we detach from our thoughts and become their observer. In the beginning of this practice, it is hard to resist being pulled into a stream of thoughts and begin thinking but it is possible to do this even for a few seconds. Even within a few seconds we become aware of the space that exists before a new thought arrives. Here the true reality stands revealed:

There exists an awareness outside of thought that is the observer of thoughts and anything else that it is focused upon

Our thoughts come to us but they are not us

Our awareness of our own thoughts can reduce their flow and our awareness can detach from our thoughts altogether

Within traditional meditation we recognise that Universal Awareness simply exists without the need for thinking. We let go of the need for thoughts until meditation becomes largely free of them. In this state of being we find deep peace and a sense of divine connection which is what Universal Awareness really is, our divine self connected to the totality of the Divine itself. Now this is where it gets really interesting. In this experience we get a sense of potentiality as though our awareness has the potential to go to another level which is undefined. This is the area of spiritual growth that is largely uncharted as many spiritual writers and teachers cannot or do not explore this. Our Universal Awareness is not meant to sit still with us just in meditation or simply to operate quietly behind our personality in daily life. Ultimately it is there to lead us into expanded states of consciousness. This I will explore in the chapters on Rainbow and Diamond consciousness which are the areas where our Universal Awareness shows its true glory.

Most people meditate more than they realise. When we day dream we can enter into altered states of consciousness similar to those experienced within formal meditation. Daydreaming becomes a type of meditation. The thoughts slow down and the Universal Awareness emerges into our own awareness. Often people find inspiration and ideas whilst day dreaming as they have accessed the pure knowing of the Universal Awareness which is the source of inspiration. These episodes are often forgotten as it is difficult to remember altered states of consciousness within normal everyday consciousness where the mind and its thoughts command our full attention. Some spiritual seekers are aware of the benefit of day dreaming and it allows them space to contemplate. Contemplation is an open and receptive state where we allow divine inspiration to flow into our awareness. This state of being opens the doors of perception to the Universal Awareness in an indirect way as opposed to formal meditation which is a direct approach. Often there is no conscious decision to do this and it may happen when we are tired or simply bored with thinking.

Daydreaming is an example of the emergence of Universal Awareness in everyday life. As such the personal experience of our spirit can take place at whatever level of consciousness we are. At lower levels of consciousness this appears to happen to us in a random manner and they are brief and mystical encounters. At the higher level of Rainbow and Diamond consciousness we are an active participant in the expression of our Universal Awareness.

Of course meditation is not the only way to become aware of our Universal Awareness. If we acknowledge that Universal Awareness is spirit then we can also define it as being our eternal divine essence. As such our Universal Awareness projects divine qualities such as peace, serenity, purity, trust and truth. When a person is fully embracing their Universal Awareness, others sense this as a magical divine force radiates out from them. Perhaps this is what people have noticed when they were in the presence of Saints, Gurus and advanced spiritual seekers. Through their own Universal Awareness these people open a door to the divine for others to enter into. To witness the Universal Awareness in another is to allow yourself to connect to your own experience of Universal Awareness. This is why there have always been spiritual teachers who embody divine qualities as a living example to others of the divine realities made manifest in the physical world. Humanity has always sought physical proofs and confirmations of divine realities and it is through the grace of those genuine spiritual teachers that many have found this. The mistake that some spiritual seekers make is to assume that they can only access the divine universal awareness through another such as spiritual teacher. This is not an empowered approach and good spiritual teachers will always point the spiritual seeker back to themselves and give them the tools to access their spirit by themselves.

Our own Universal Awareness resonates with universal spirit that reveals its presence in the physical world. When this happens we are attracted to something because it has an inexplicable sense of wonder about it. The beauty of a sunset, the perfection of nature or the enjoyment that music brings are all examples of this. The sense of wonder we have for such things is our Universal Awareness recognising divine qualities that it resonates with and that stand out in the mundane world. As such we can use our sense of wonder as a tool to access our own Universal Awareness. If you recognise something in this world that fascinates you and brings about a sense of wonder then you can allow yourself to focus on it. This usually slows down our thoughts and draws our awareness from the outer world to the inner world which is the home of Universal Awareness. This allows us to communicate with spirit through the language of the Universal Awareness which is pure knowing.

Another example of a scenario where the Universal Awareness emerges into our experience is when we experience a deep disturbance of a mental and emotional nature. With unexpected events our personal identity is challenged. Perhaps someone loses their job or partner and this brings questions about the future and their identity if they did not have these things. At the personality level, and within lower levels of consciousness our self identity is mainly constructed by the negative ego and it is directly affected by surprising events which can temporarily disarm it. For a short time there is a complete absence of its normal responses and negative emotions. We then become strongly aware of our Universal Awareness which is experienced as unmistakable peace and clarity of perception. When the illusions of the negative ego come crashing down, truth and expanded awareness are revealed to us by our spirit. This can last for an instant or longer. Often when someone "hits rock bottom" this is what they experience, the illumination of the true reality. Many spiritual seekers will tell you about their "awakening" which often comes about after some type of negative experience which allowed them to have such revelations. Spiritual growth often comes after such challenges and suffering. Often disturbing events act as the catalyst for growth as it helps us come face to face with our negative ego. In those dark moments the light of the Universal Awareness dissolves aspects of the negative ego. The depth of truth that is revealed by the Universal Awareness is hard to deny and fundamentally changes us. We realise this truth which means that we sense it with every fibre of our being. This pattern is continued up until the level of Crystal Consciousness when we realise that we can choose a different pattern of growth. In higher consciousness we are more aware of the operations and workings of the components of our human condition. It is natural to want to have a more enjoyable experience of spiritual growth and so we seek to resist this process of transformation less than previously. We search willingly for that which is needed to take us to the next level. We then become willing participants of our growth patterns at a personality level. This is called the path of Grace as we grow in a more graceful manner. Spiritual growth does not have to be all about hard work and suffering. These are the experiences at lower levels of consciousness where the path of grace is not known. Indeed at the higher levels of Crystal and Rainbow consciousness, spiritual growth becomes more of a process of allowance. It is easier than before as there is less resistance and it can be an exquisite and blissful as we merge with the love and light of the Universe. The path of Grace is all about deeper levels of surrender which allow the true beauty and power of the Universe to be revealed to us.

Transcending the negative ego with Universal Awareness

When we allow the Light of Universal Awareness into our conscious experience, this dissolves the illusions of the negative ego. This allows us to transcend much of the negative ego in a powerful and quick way. In higher consciousness there is less need for processes to take a long time and to be arduous. Even in short periods of connection to Universal Awareness we move our identification towards oneness and away from the ego. This dissolved the negative ego. As such a short meditation or a deep realisation along these lines is in many ways more powerful than the practice of a thousand affirmations or the reading of spiritual books.

How to deliberately embody Universal Awareness / Spirit

We experience Universal Awareness during meditation or in brief glimpses that occur in seemingly random moments whilst we day dream and contemplate. Some even come to recognise the experience of Universal Awareness as being important and deeply satisfying. They want more and so the process of identifying with spirit deepens. When we start to identify with these experiences as being a part of "me" and a preferred way of being then we start to bring spirit into this world. People are the channels for Spirit / Universal Awareness into the physical world. When we embrace this deep spiritual reality we embody it. I have an exercise that I use in workshops that illustrates this point well. I ask participants to connect to Universal Awareness / Spirit in meditation. They usually have experiences of peace, expanded awareness and a sense of unlimited potential. These are the typical experiences of Spirit. I then ask them to perform the same exercise and this time to acknowledge Universal Awareness by simply saying, "hello" to it within their meditation. The result is that the energies of the room rise incredibly as the participants really connect to spirit and bring its presence to our earthly level of awareness. With this simple gesture we learn the true nature of Spirit which is that it is INTERACTIVE and intelligent. Universal Awareness is waiting to reveal itself to us at whatever level we are prepared to engage it. By signalling in a meditation that we are open to being interactive with spirit we allow it to reach into our experience. It is not only in formal meditation that we experience spirit. Certainly within Rainbow and Diamond levels of consciousness, our awareness is more fluid and life becomes more like a walking meditation where we experience frequent altered states of consciousness. It is within these altered states of consciousness that we attract more experiences of spirit as our conscious relationship with it grows and develops. At this stage we can connect in awareness to spirit simply by willing this to be. This could be at any time or in any place. And so connecting to Universal Awareness does not have to be something we only do in a formal meditation as it is something we can do in ordinary life situations. We can bring this higher awareness into any or all situations. This can be when we are seeking an insight into something, when we need the comfort of spiritual connection, or when we are trying to serve others and we wish to be a channel of spirit in whatever way we can express this. I find that my connection to Universal Awareness is amplified when I give talks and workshops. It seems the opportunity to connect to others attracts the interactive nature of spirit more than anything else! I invite ascension seekers to explore and experiment with Universal Awareness. If you want it to be in your conscious human experience then you must invite it in! If you want to share it with others then find ways to do this. The more we do this the more Universal Awareness becomes our way of being and we ground it into this world. It is no longer a spiritual experience that exists solely in meditation or random experiences.

A person embodying Spirit has a magnetic quality to them which is very mysterious and attractive to others. Others strongly recognise the essence of Spirit around those who embody it. Such ascension seekers represent doorways to the divine through which others can be connected to deeper spiritual realities. Being in the presence of such a person can activate all kinds of healing and spiritual experiences in ordinary people. Such is the power and potential of Universal Awareness / Spirit. This has been witnessed with saints, gurus and spiritual teachers throughout the ages. I say this not to present ascension seekers as being important but to highlight the potentials that exist for us to help others in profound ways when we allow spirit to flow through us.

The language of the Universal Awareness

If the Universal Awareness does not present itself to us in thought patterns then how does it communicate to us? It communicates to us using our INNER SENSES. These are not physical senses but spiritual senses that allow us to be aware of non physical spiritual realities and our own inner working as a complex being. Here are some of them.

The sense of Knowing

When we know something there is no doubt about it. What is the colour of your house or car? You simply know the answer to these questions. There is no need to think about it or analyse it. It is what it is. There is no thinking taking place. Imagine knowing the answer to a lot of things and especially about spiritual realities. This is how the Universal Awareness speaks to us in a clear, calm and deep ways. It allows us to know without having to think. We have realisations where we know something at a deep enough level that it is felt at every level of our being. Where we present a desire to know something either consciously or unconsciously, then the Universal Awareness shares its awareness with us in that area to the degree that we are able to know it. Our Universal Awareness is connected to the Universal Awareness of everything and so we are joined with the awareness of God which knows everything. Of course our thoughts inevitably become involved and it is fine if we want to reflect on what we have experienced through knowing. If we want to think about it afterwards this can lead to an understanding at the conscious level as the mind seeks to build new models of understanding at a more everyday human level. Indeed this is how we build our own language with the Universal Awareness as it reveals more to us. In the initial stages of this language not all things can be known as there are degrees to knowing. With any realisation we can always go deeper. As we grow we learn how to go deeper. Each new realisation leads to others which create ever expanding models of understanding. In the early experiences of Universal Awareness what we realise is true but additional layers of truth await the arrival of our awareness.

The Sense of freedom / lightness

Freedom is registered by us as lightness in our mood and emotions. There is a lack of anxiety and pressure which are normally caused when we feel trapped by the negative emotions, thoughts and situations of life. We are peaceful and free of burdens. There is "space" in our awareness and this often allows us to connect to the energies and inspiration of creativity. New ideas, solutions or artistic projects are born into this space. Often we have glimpses of this sense of freedom and lightness immediately after a period of letting go of obligations and limitations of any kind. However it is limited as we revert back to the tendency of feeling trapped and powerless in daily life.

The Sense of Vibration

Everything has a sense of vibration that is unique and we can detect these vibrations. All life has vibration as it describes the spiritual essence of all things. Even "objects" such as stones and flowers have vibration.

The sense of multi dimensional spiritual realities

It is possible to sense spiritual energies and consciousness itself. These are certainly not physical senses. Different dimensions of consciousness exist outside of the physical universe and we are a part of those realms too. In a sense it is that part of us that exists in the relevant format in that realm can communicate to a part of our awareness anchored to the physical body. These can be subtle and if developed can describe the qualities of spiritual energies and consciousness.

The Sense of Bliss, Ecstasy and Joy

In our deepest spiritual experiences we encounter Bliss and Ecstasy. These are more than human emotions and can be described as magical moments when we align ourselves to the greatest purpose of the Universe and become one with it. The human sexual organism is an obvious example of this where sexual intercourse becomes the deliberate of act of co-creation with the Universe.

Joy is a state of being that radiates out of us expressing deep contentment as we realise that we are also divine as well as being human. It is felt is the higher heart of the higher heart area.

The Sense of truth

Truth is more than accurate information as it is also describes the way information is communicated in a manner that is free of illusions, personal agendas, and lies. Through the sense of Truth we can tell when a communication is pure (free of distortion) and we sense how it reflects the true universal reality. Virtually all people distort the true nature of things within their personal realities as the cause of this distortion is the ego which in most people is unchecked. However God/ The Universe does not have an ego and so communication directly from God / The Universe is free of these distortions and is experienced as pure, holy and important. When an individual has transcended their ego then they too communicate and express themselves in ways that are largely free of ego. This is noticeable by others who recognise the Truth in their expressions.

The Sense of Purity

In a similar way purity is recognised as the original divine content or expression of something free of human illusions, corruption and distortions.

The sense of Meaning and Purpose

Whether they are aware of it or not, everybody is searching for meaning and purpose to life. Those who are spiritually orientated realise that this search goes beyond the material things in life and is therefore a spiritual quest to find meaning and purpose in life.

The greatest sense of meaning and purpose a human being can experience comes about when we are aware of our personal connection to God / The Universe and when we are willing and conscious participants in this alignment. The sense of meaning is not so much an emotion but rather it is a state of being. We have meaning in our life or we do not. We are "being" meaning or we are not. When we experience the sense of meaning, it brings about the senses of unlimited joy, completeness and belonging that nothing in the physical world can. Not only can we detect the sense of meaning and we can detect its absence which is caused by a lack of a conscious spiritual connection and is felt as boredom, frustration and depression.

Another more insightful definition of meaning is the nearer we are to God / The Universe the more meaning we sense and enjoy. There are degrees to the sense of meaning. As such the sense of meaning can act as a measurement to how much we are spiritually aligned. The deeper we move into the energy and consciousness of God / The Universe the deeper the sense of meaning we experience. Our Universal Awareness communicates this to us through the inner sense of meaning. This becomes important in the levels of Rainbow and Diamond Consciousness where we actively exercise our Universal Awareness by projecting it into larger fields of universal energy and consciousness. This is the act of expanding our own consciousness and exploring higher levels of universal love and intelligence. Here the sense of meaning guides us to higher and more pure levels of consciousness. This is the journey away from humanity towards the divine.

The sense of Realisation

When we realise something we know it with every fibre of our being. We are not thinking it but rather we know about it in a full way. There is no analysis taking place here and there are no doubts. Moments of realisation are inspired moments where communication comes from the universe. It could be a solution to a problem or the deeper understanding of something. Our intuition often is the communication system that allows moments of realisation.

A Model of Ascension

Problems with existing ascension models and teachings

Each generation creates its own models of spiritual understanding and ascension based on its level of consciousness at that time. The work of Madam Blavatsky, Alice Bailey and the Theosophy movement is excellent and has formed the foundation for the understanding of ascension for many years. However the presentation and flavour of this work makes it increasingly hard for modern spiritual seekers to relate to. It reflects the mood of society at that time and represents an occult approach which is peppered with rules and is obsessed with hierarchies. This is not so helpful at this time where the need is to let go of limitation of all kinds. During the 1990's the new age movement brought out updated ascension teachings that give more inspiration, hope and a sense of personal responsibility and personal power. This was perfect for that time as it supported the movement of energy and consciousness which can be described as the drive for transformation of self and society and the search for higher truth. This was chiefly a mental approach and was part of the Indigo level of consciousness. However this approach also has its limitations as it can be too mental. It does not ideally support the transition to the higher levels of consciousness starting with Crystal Consciousness which requires the surrender of the lower mind in favour of the heart approach. Specifically the teachings of that time rely heavily on Initiation levels and light quotient levels which are technical measurements of ascension expressed in terms of percentages. Whilst these are useful to measure the progress of ascension, this information can only be collected by good channels. As such it not a very empowered approach for those working on ascension as unless they can continually employ channels to provide this information, they will not be able to monitor their ascension progress with these models. For some the act of reducing the totality of their consciousness to a single number is too limiting and hard to relate to. What are needed now are methods for individuals to personally monitor their own ascension progress in easy and recognisable ways. This can be achieved by learning to listen to our own thoughts, emotions and inner senses which give us feedback on current levels of consciousness within ascension. The path of ascension leads us to become an ascended master and a master of self. This means being a master of our own thoughts, emotions and energies. It is inconceivable that such mastery would not include the ability to perceive what level of ascension we personally are at. As such in my writing I seek to offer the insights and approaches which help others to be more aware of their current levels of consciousness as well as where they are heading within their growth patterns.

I have created a model of ascension that can be used as a map for all ascension seekers. It seeks to show the reader the following information:

Personal and current levels of ascension

Our emotions, thoughts and inner senses are constantly giving us feedback on our own level of consciousness. Through the act of monitoring these we can see patterns and qualities. We then use these insights as markers which describe our level of consciousness. I have used the following model to describe specific information on each of seven higher levels of consciousness that are experienced within the ascension journey. This includes the type of spiritual growth patterns, spiritual lessons, emotional experiences and the use of the intellect. Certain phases will resonate with individuals are they are able to recognise the descriptions as being currently relevant to their own experiences of life and spirituality. You can use this information as a map to show you continually show you where you are in the process. You will strongly identify with the content one or two of these levels and this is your confirmation that is your current level of consciousness.

What are the core spiritual agendas for any specific phase of ascension?

What are the challenges at specific levels and phases of ascension? Each level has its specific core spiritual agenda that need to be engaged before an ascension seeker can move to the next level. It is crucial that ascension seekers understand the core spiritual agenda that faces them at all times. Not to do this would result in confusion and lost opportunities. In the table below these are described as the areas of learning. The area called "perfecting" refers to the lessons of the previous phase which we continue to practice and integrate in the new higher level.

How to move to the next level of ascension

Each level of ascension has a specific area of human lower consciousness that has to be let go of or surrendered. Successful completion of this spiritual task helps us to rise to the next level. However the inability to complete the requirements for letting go and surrendering actually traps an individual at the same level. This can be a frustrating and confusing experience as that individual will continually attract to them the same spiritual lessons in life which are related to the surrender issue.

A summary of this model is below and the information is fully described and explained in the individual studies of each phase and level of ascension.

	Indigo (personal Power)	Indigo (Intellect)	Crystal (love)	Crystal (Joy)	Rainbow	Diamond
Perfecting	Personal Power	Spiritual intelligence	Acceptance	Self love	Non – attachment	Divine Surrender
Learning	Spiritual intelligence	Acceptance	Self love	Non – attachment	Divine Surrender	Grace
Master Teacher		Dr Joshua Stone	Jesus Christ	Buddha	Mary Magdalene	The Universe
Alignment to	human personality	human mind	soul	soul + spirit	spirit	spirit

The progression of ascension can be described as the journey through distinct levels of consciousness where each new level represents a higher level of consciousness as illustrated below.

Negative Ego / spiritually inactive

↓

Indigo (including the two distinct phases of personal power & intellect / mind)

↓

Crystal (including the two distinct phases of unconditional love & unconditional joy)

↓

Rainbow (peace)

↓

Diamond (transcendence)

↓

Ascension (completion)

Examples

Each phase and level of ascension also presents its own spiritual growth patterns and lessons. At each level we automatically attract these specific growth opportunities into our lives and so daily life becomes our teacher and guide. These are often challenges that help us to master the themes of the phase that we are in and help us to move onto higher phases and levels. All you have to do is make a note of the common and consistent lessons / growth themes you are noticing in your life and use the notes from my map to place yourself in the right level.

Are these...

Power struggles, the need to stand up for yourself and speak your truth? If you are consistently attracting these experiences then you are most likely to be at the Indigo Level and within the personal power phase.

Are you reading many spiritual books and attending many spiritual workshops in order to deeply understand yourself and spirituality in general? Is this process extremely important for you right now? Are you not quite satisfied with what you already know and are you getting a bit frustrated with this process? If these are your common experiences then you are most likely to be at the Indigo Level and in the mind / intellect phase.

Are you learning to really love and to forgive others? Do you desperately want to connect to spiritual realities in intimate and deep ways? If these are your common experiences then you are most likely to be at the Crystal Level and in the unconditional love phase.

Are you seeking more peace and isolation in life? Do you meditate and daydream more than ever? Are you becoming more intuitive, physic and empathic just now? If these are your common experiences then you are most likely to be at the Rainbow level of consciousness.

Notes for this model

The Generic descriptions of Indigo, Crystal and Rainbow came about as certain people noticed a difference in the auric fields of those with higher consciousness. The names given were in part descriptions of the colours and appearance of these auric fields. I use the terms not to draw attention to the appearance of specific auric fields, but rather to focus on specific bands of human spiritual consciousness. It is not necessary to see auras in order to use the model and descriptions that I use.

This is a model of ascension that I use that reflects my level of consciousness and my experiences. As with all models it can be changed and indeed as we all continue to raise our consciousness I have no doubt that other models will emerge. This model does not represent the only truth or the ultimate truth. It is a tool for us to use now which we can replace with a more useful model in the future. It is important not to get too attached to any spiritual models or teachings as this can prevent our growth if we insist on hanging onto them when new ideas and practices become necessary.

It is possible to straddle two phases as we make a transition from one level to the next higher one. This explains why some ascension seekers are drawn to the descriptions of two phases.

This progression is not strictly linear. This means that it is possible to move to a higher level of ascension without completing all of the lessons of the previous phase. Inevitably this would need to be completed later on and we all periodically revisit parts of the agendas of previous levels.

It is possible to fall to a lower level of conscious at any time. Consciousness is fluid and can fall as well as rise. We all need to be aware of this and to monitor our own consciousness. When we find that we have slipped back into old ways of thinking and behaviour it can result in our consciousness falling. A Master continually monitors this situation and when necessary takes steps to raise their consciousness back to its previous highest level.

As we progress in the ascension process we add new levels of expanded consciousness to previous levels. We do not remove previous levels. For example someone moving from Indigo (intellect) to Crystal level Unconditional love will still retain within their consciousness the abilities and positive qualities of Indigo. From time to time they will need to use the developed intellect of the Indigo phases or to stand in their power when they are challenged. These qualities will not leave them as they move into higher levels. However it is likely that in the new higher levels they will adopt different ways of being that are more suited to higher levels of consciousness and so the Indigo flavours will fade until they are needed to be called on.

Indigo Consciousness - Intellectual Exploration

Key experiences and motivations

Drive for transformation of self and society

Search for higher truth and information

Search for personal identity

Challenging nature and rejection of the status quo

Specific Phases of Indigo Experience

Phase of consciousness	Actual Experience	Key attributes needed	Challenges at this level	Surrender required for next level
Pride	negative thoughts, emotions and behaviour as negative ego is uncontrolled. Arrogance, stubbornness and defensiveness.	recognising the negative ego in operation within self, beginning to know difference between truth and illusion, humility and humour	limited spiritual growth, disharmony in relationships, suffering	the realisation that we are not perfect and change is needed
Personal Power	Seeking change in life even when there is resistance to this, standing up for our needs,	empowerment, integrity, self development, will, fortitude, determination, courage and ability to surrender	challenges of being true to self when not supported by friends, family, society etc	the need to personally control things, reluctunce to trust in the divine
Reason / lower mind / intellect	clarity of thought, intelligence, search for spiritual truth, identity and meaning	appreciation for spiritual truth and wisdom, clear understanding about oneself,	tendency for rigid mind set, need to remain open to new models of understanding and new experiences	surrender to the heart, no longer needing to experience spirituality through the mind, Acceptance of all things in our life

A good example of Indigo consciousness is shown by the rock and pop stars of the 1960's, 1970's and 1980's. They were seekers of change in society. Normal life was insufficient for them and they sought new experiences and higher ways of being. They do not like what they saw in the world around them and they were instinctively motivated to adopt different values and lifestyles. These Indigos encouraged change all around them. This desire to challenge society is common amongst Indigos. They instinctively know that humans can be much more and they see evolution as natural and even easy. Their beliefs are reflected in their lyrics, lifestyles and philosophies. Humans are slow to evolve and so many of these Indigos experienced resistance from society to their cause. In their desperate search for new ways some of these musicians experimented with drugs, sex and alternative lifestyles. Nothing was off limits to them. Their greatest spiritual contribution was to encourage society to challenge the status quo and authority. Even if they were consciously unaware of what they were doing they succeeded in helping others to become more independent in their thinking. And so the 1960's-1990's became the time of great development in independent thinking and especially within the spiritual new age movement. An intellectual approach to spirituality was thoroughly explored and perfected. However there is a new requirement for humanity now to evolve beyond the Indigo experience and towards the Crystal consciousness. Those that hold Crystal Consciousness are the new leaders for humanity but they are very different from the Indigo rock and pop stars!

In some ways I miss the passion and the uniqueness of those Indigos. They brought so much inspiration to me and many others. Their ability to create new forms of music was incredible. They were so creative and so talented. Currently music is so bland in comparison. Current Rock and pop stars are often guilty of copying the Indigos of the previous generations but they lack that Indigo soul.

Phases of Indigo Consciousness

Pride

At this level a person is incapable of discerning between truth from falsehood and they confuse perception with reality. This level of consciousness is defensive and vulnerable as the individual is dependent on external conditions to overcome fear and insecurities. Pride becomes a defence and self-esteem is built on exaggerated and inflated opinion rather than reality. The solution is to move towards self-approval rather than to constantly seek approval from others.

There is no capacity to understand non-linear experience and so personal consciousness is limited. Normal expressions and motivations include always wanting to be right, blaming others, seeking admiration and getting even. Humility and integrity are needed to progress to the next phase of consciousness – Personal Power. It may surprise people that I have included this in the Indigo section as Indigo is considered to be an evolved level of consciousness. Pride is not a level of Indigo but I have included it for good reason. Our personal consciousness can fall down in levels as well as to rise in levels. Most people experience temporary periods where their consciousness descends. As such it may happen that someone normally operating from the level of Personal Power or higher is challenged in life in such a way that they revert to a previous lower level such as the level of Pride. I have included this paragraph so that this level is recognisable and therefore we can all take positive steps to raise our consciousness if we find ourselves at this level. Even a somewhat evolved or enlightened spiritual person can experience the level of Pride as well as the lower levels.

Personal Power

This is the major positive phase of ascension where personal power is explored and mastered. Personal power is about recognising truth as well as speaking and living your truth. Personal responsibility is taken for developing and integrating higher qualities into the personality including empowerment, integrity, self-development, will, the ability to surrender, fortitude, determination, courage and the ability to surrender. It is the major turning point in ascension where many negative habits and thoughts are given up in favour of higher habits and thoughts. Within this phase there is significant progress made in transcending fear and the negative ego. Here self-improvement is sought through spiritual, energetic and psychological therapies. This is the time when we make life changing decisions. We become less influenced by those around us as we courageously choose positive courses of action for ourselves. Often this results in a loss of those things that hold us back. Old relationships, occupations and interests are typically exchanged for new and more appropriate ones. It is the time for outer transformation and the sowing of the seeds for great inner transformation to come.

Intellect / lower mind – This is the experience of consciousness where there is a great progress made in the search for spiritual truth, personal identity and meaning. Intelligence and clarity of thought are developed. Truth emerges. This comes about as more of the negative ego has been transcended. This means that the distortions of truth by the negative ego are less prevalent making clear recognition of spiritual truths and realities more possible. There is a false assumption by many that this level of consciousness is the highest level possible. This is because it is extremely hard to imagine what lies beyond this. The next level of consciousness (Crystal) represents a new paradigm where human consciousness is experienced in a vastly different way. As such there is a great need for us to understand that the essential requirement at the Indigo Intellect Level is to surrender to the heart and to no longer need to largely experience spirituality through the mind. This does not mean that we will never use the mind again, but rather that we recognise that this is only one of many ways of perceiving our experiences. Further levels of consciousness offer more mystical experiences that are beyond the ability of the mind to comprehend and exceed the ability of language to describe.

To surrender to the heart is to **ACCEPT** things as they are. When we learn to accept everything including our dark side then we are heading for a new and expanded appreciation of life through Crystal consciousness. To accept things does not mean to live a life with no opinions or plans. It means that we longer fight or resist things. We no longer react to situations but we respond to them instead. We practice acceptance, compassion, forgiveness and we develop wisdom. This leads to freedom and liberation from human polarised thinking such as right / wrong and good / bad. Examples of the practice of acceptance are:

We accept that our mind will never understand everything and especially spiritual realities

We accept the faults in our self and others without insisting on anyone being perfect

We accept spiritual lessons and their value even when this takes us out of our comfort zones or clashes with our plans

We accept that in order to grow and transform we must change aspects of self which hold this process back

Acceptance leads to love as when we accept something we are more open to seeing its beauty and purpose. We learn to love which is the experience of crystal consciousness. Acceptance includes forgiveness. Forgiveness is the letting go of power struggles in favour of wanting harmony and trusting love will show us he way.

A deep understanding of true forgiveness is that we realise that it releases us from the harm which your negative attitudes and energies cause to you. True forgiveness is not dependent on other people doing anything specific such as apologising, understanding our point of view or accepting blame. True forgiveness comes when we cease viewing ourselves as victims and take action to change our attitudes because we value freedom, harmony and love.

At this level it feels as if we are in a spiritual "limbo". This is a type of spiritual growth holding pattern. We recognise that we no longer possess many of the old patterns of thinking and behaviour but also that we have not yet arrived at an indefinable level of being that we are searching for. What they are unconsciously searching for is the way of the heart. This can be a very frustrating process as it feels like we are moving somewhere and yet not necessarily knowing where you are moving to. This situation remains until there is a surrender of the mind in favour of the heart which begins the next higher level of consciousness called Crystal Consciousness. This is hard as it requires the letting go of assumptions, habits and models of understanding that may have existed for someone's whole adult life. It is also a step into the unknown and a move away from normal human experience behaviour towards higher consciousness.

Identification as experienced within the Indigo levels of human consciousness

After a spiritual awakening some enter into the Indigo level of consciousness. An awakened spiritual seeker (Indigo) identifies with their thoughts and their emotional responses to the world around them. They are seeking deeper understandings to their spiritual and philosophical questions. Here less importance is placed on the physical and materialistic worlds. Identification is now switching from the physical world outside of self to the inner worlds of thought, contemplation, and emotion. "I" becomes not just a physical being but also a being with a spiritual component mainly experienced through the intellect but also through emotions and occasional mystical experiences. In relation to the world around us, "I" appears to be an individual but with a growing sense of a mystical connection to the world and universe that is yet to be defined or fully explored.

How transcendence of the negative ego is experienced within Indigo Consciousness - Personal Power

In all types of new age and cognitive therapies there is recognition that our thoughts influence our emotions. Negative thought patterns produce negative emotions which are unpleasant and cause suffering. The ego creates fear and illusion. Until the negative ego is transcended then people will continually experience negative enotions.

The drive at this level is to reform self and so ascension seekers explore all kinds of self help programmes and healing therapies. This is setting up the powerful intention to transform self which is a triumph over the fear of the ego. At this stage there are unlikely to be any experiences of universal awareness yet. However momentum can be built up which can take individuals to the next level in consciousness. It is interesting to observe those whose consciousness is below the level of personal power which is the first of the spiritual levels of consciousness. Here their ego thrives and the individual is not consciously aware of its existence. The mere suggestion of a healing session will be met with refusal. Their ego knows that this is a path that could eventually lead to its own destruction and so even irrational behaviour will be used to avoid such possibilities.

Popular methods of reprogramming our conscious and sub-conscious thoughts make use of affirmations and visualisations. These are simple techniques which promote positive thoughts and in turn can lead to positive emotions. Affirmations are positive statements that are repeated and visualizations are positive images that are used in meditation. In the phase of personal power these are good techniques that allow us to take responsibility for the state of our consciousness and we want to "do" things that help us to evolve. These techniques loosen the grip of the ego somewhat but they do not get to the core spiritual agenda which is the need to let go of controlling approaches and to be accepting. There is also a question about which affirmations are chosen as the negative ego in this phase is still functioning and influencing. If someone is choosing affirmations to transform only those areas in life that bring comfort to the personality and they do little to challenge that negative ego itself then very little evolution will take place. For example if the major focus of spiritual activity is placed on attracting financial abundance then an individual may focus themselves with this issue when the core areas of activity needed to transcend the negative ego are not addressed. What serves our personality is not always what serves our true spiritual development.

Indigo - Mind / Intellect

At the level of Indigo Mind / Intellect we are aware of the negative ego as a concept. We try to observe it in operation as it influences our thoughts and emotions. The art of self enquiry is practiced. Our Universal Awareness is experienced in rare but powerful events. When this happens the negative ego is clearly exposed and mini triumphs are achieved in transcending the negative ego. However the negative ego uses the mind to justify its existence and to also to encourage distraction and confusion. At this level as the mind is trying to think its way out of negativity and it is looking to understand everything. The nature of the mind is that it analyses and debates. It is constantly receiving new information and so it is never satisfied as it is always searching for something new to analyse. It is simply not possible for the mind to achieve full control through understanding the negative ego within its own terms of reference. Classic Indigos at this stage will believe that more is better and so they will continue to look for the all important information that will finally satisfy the conscious mind and bring it the control that it seeks. More books, courses and Gurus are explored and probed within the search for the elusive material. The negative ego encourages this as although this approach forms a logical strategy, it is actually avoiding what is needed to progress. Within the struggle to achieve this, the ego influences us to fall into despair and to feel frustration and anger. This leads to apathy where the negative ego is safe. Many spiritual students give up trying at this stage and go in stasis. They remove themselves from further spiritual activity temporarily or even permanently. They conclude that it is not possible to intellectually understand what they desire to know and so become fatigued in their efforts. Their ascension to Crystal Consciousness is delayed or abandoned.

In this phase of consciousness it is appropriate that the intellect is developed and that Spirituality is explored through the mind. However the human mind alone is incapable of understanding complex spiritual realities. Our universal awareness does understand spiritual realities though but at this level the mind is too engaged in thinking to realise this. If acceptance is to be found within the intellect then it is to accept that the mind cannot fully understand all spiritual realities and that it is necessary to give up with this requirement. Our conscious mind has to simply accept that some things are unknowable for the mind and that we can experience spiritual realities in other ways. When we crave deeper spiritual experiences more than we crave the intellectual understanding of spirituality then we allow ourselves to find new ways to evolve. When we want to "be" more than we want to "do" we allow evolution to take us to the next level.

When we give up trying to change others and society in an Indigo fashion then we find acceptance. This does not mean that we do not care about things but rather than we no longer insist on approaching change in the Indigo way. We remove ourselves from the struggle of saving an imperfect world. We accept that people are as they are. Why do we do this? The movement to change others and society demands that we engage in challenging thoughts and behaviour and we are perpetually in conflict with the world around us. The negative ego of course loves conflict and thrives in this environment. As such in the Indigo level we must always ask our self if the motivation for challenge is a genuine desire for transformation or if sometimes it is the disguised expression of our negative ego. Whilst it is possible to transform ourselves we find that it is impossible to transform others unless they are willing for this to happen. This Indigo style brings little to us personally in terms of love or meaningful spiritual experiences. We begin to sense the lack of these experiences and we crave them. When this situation is acute enough we realise that we must change course and operate in a different way. We then desire love and harmony more than confrontation and "being right". We enter into universal acceptance of all things. With this new state of being we are not condoning negativity behaviour or ignorance but rather we choose to see beyond such things in search of genuine spiritual relationships to people and life itself. We have disarmed the negative ego somewhat and we have taken responsibility for our experiences. When practicing acceptance we can more easily see the beauty and positive aspects of ourselves and others. We become more compassionate and the heart opens. This is the entrance into Crystal Consciousness - the way of the heart and unconditional love. Love becomes more unconditional as we accept the faults of others rather than to insist that they are one way or another. Of course this also applies to our self. When we accept our self now without condition and with all of our imperfections, we feel compassion and allow a deep understanding of self to emerge. We feel self love.

These are the Core Spiritual Agendas needed to be realised at the Indigo phase in order to allow entrance into Crystal Consciousness.

The Master Teachers of Indigo (Intellect) are the experts on the human mind, spiritual psychology and cogniative therapies such as Dr Joshua D. Stone and David R. Hawkins.

Crystal Consciousness - Emotional Exploration

Key experiences and motivations

- An open heart
- A total acceptance of self, others and the way the world is - Forgiveness
- loving and nurturing attitude to people, animals, plants, environment and all things spiritual
- Expanded awareness, awareness of spiritual energies & realities, empathic, telepathic and psychic tendencies – ability to know other people at deeper levels
- Higher consciousness and a healing presence
- The desire for more oneness and peace rather than being judgmental and wanting to be right
- Avoidance of negative energies, people and situations. This is discernment and not judgement
- Lots of eye contact and affection
- Humble attitude – less ego

Phases of Crystal Consciousness

Unconditional love

Key words: Acceptance, Gratitude, Embrace, Forgiveness, Nurture, Expansion, Caring, Appreciation, Unconditional, Intuition & Empathic

phase of consciousness	actual experience	key attributes needed	challenges at this level	surrender required for next level
Unconditional love	loving and nurturing attitude, expanded awareness, higher consciousness and a healing presence,	an open heart, acceptance of things as they are, realisation of new way of being in this new paradigm	to avoid closing heart in difficult situations, to be unconditional, understanding that unconditional love is not romantic love	love self and embrace inner divine presence, recognise God in self as well as outside of self

A "Crystal"

The type of person that embodies the qualities of Crystal Consciousness in the most obvious ways is a healer. All Crystals are healers as their presence is healing to others. However there are those Crystals who have the opportunity to work as an energetic healer, complementary therapist or counsellor and so for me these are good examples. They have an open heart and they simply wish to help others even when their own needs are not being met. Their healing gifts become a focus for service work. Unconditional love becomes the motivation for their efforts. These Crystals are popular as everyone likes to bathe in their wonderful auras. They exude kindness, appreciation and acceptance of others. We do not feel judged by them but loved by them. It is these qualities that make them good healers. People are able to trust them and open up to them. Healing and transformation is then more likely. These Crystals personify the teachings of Jesus Christ. He taught the "way of the heart" through learning to accept, forgive and love others unconditionally. He spoke the language of Crystals two thousand years ago and so I have nominated him as the Master of Crystal Consciousness.

Whilst some individual advanced ascension seekers will achieve Crystal consciousness and higher in this lifetime, it is the destiny of humanity to ascend its consciousness too. If most of humanity were to achieve the Crystal level of consciousness, then most of the global problems of war, greed and corruption would eventually be solved. The qualities of Crystals are such that they cannot tolerate such negativity and so they would not support them anything that promotes such things. The Crystal approach of serving others would facilitate the necessary changes that would ensure this transformation of humanity. However it would not be a transformation that is imposed on others and which is unpopular. It would be a transformation that expresses the genuine desires of Crystals and is recognised by the majority as being the right approach. It must be the goal of humanity to raise it consciousness to the level of crystal consciousness. Whilst this may seem ambitious or even unobtainable, I must state that consciousness itself can be fluid and can be transformed deeply in shorter periods of time than many would assume is possible.

The motivations for moving from Indigo consciousness (personal power and intellect levels) to Crystal consciousness come about when we want to experience a real personal relationship to the divine. At previous levels within Indigo consciousness it was enough to explore spirituality and the divine in intellectual ways. Here we read about and study spirituality and our relationship to the divine chiefly takes place within the human mind. In Indigo levels we seek to understand the divine through our minds. Progress can be made with this, however this does not satisfy our yearnings to have real and tangible spiritual experiences. At some point we give up the intellectual approach as it we reach the limits of what it has to offer. The human mind was never made to understand the divine. To do this we need to move into the crystal consciousness and the way of the heart. This is the first expanded level of consciousness where we can really and consistently *sense and feel* the divine. As we move in this direction we tend to read about spirituality less and have our own spiritual experiences instead. We meditate more as it is within meditation that we become more aware of the divine.

Unconditional love - Unconditional love is much more than a loving feeling. Our energy fields become more aligned with the vast energy fields and consciousness of the universe. As such it is a high way of being that influences our entire experience of life. This includes or thoughts, emotions, energies, occupation and our relationships. It is an approach to life that seeks to be grateful, to embrace and to heal. This level of being is expressed through an open heart, with a loving and nurturing attitude to everything that we encounter.

We use the word "Unconditional" at the Crystals level as it refers to the desire that we have to maintain an open heart and loving experience in whatever circumstance we find ourselves in. In other words we do not insist that others are nice to us before we are loving. We do not insist that our lives work out the way that we want before we become loving people. For those at this level their experience of unconditional love is so precious that they never want to lose it. As such it becomes more important than what is happening in daily life. Love therefore has no conditions in life because it is a state of being that we insist on experiencing.

Please understand that I am not talking about allowing others to treat us badly. It is not being loving to ourselves to allow this to happen and so personal power runs alongside unconditional love. In fact those at this level become discerning about what energies and situations they find themselves in as they love themselves too much to allow uncomfortable or painful experiences to needlessly happen. This is not being judgmental just as it is not being judgmental to avoid anything that is harmful for us at a physical or emotional level.

Expansion

Love unites and attracts and so we are drawn to beauty, nature, people, animals as well as spiritual realities such as our soul and the Universe at large. There comes about a growing and intense desire to connect with spiritual levels once again. Expansion takes place as we willingly make new spiritual connections in this way. Love is an energy in motion and so these spiritual experiences are active. We have a remembrance that we are a part of all of this already and so we seek re-connection to spiritual realities in ways that make us feel complete.

Expansion of awareness occurs across many levels. An expanded appreciation of the divine allows us to more deeply see its beauty, wonder and perfection all around us. We become more aware of spiritual and energetic realities. We notice more our empathic, telepathic and psychic tendencies. We develop the ability to know other people at deeper levels through an awareness of their thoughts and emotions. Compassion easily follows.

It is the start of the new paradigm where a non-linear experience introduces the realities of higher dimensions. As such time and personal spirituality take on different meanings. Spirituality becomes less linear and life flows within a multi-dimensional experience. Spirituality becomes mystical. Intuition becomes clear and a normal experience of life, allowing a regular communication system with our higher self and the Universe.

Nurturing

The negative ego and fear are largely transcended and so we become less concerned about ourselves. We live in trust and increasingly feel less separation from other people and the Universe. We sense common spiritual connections to others a reality. We feel included within the universe. We value other people more and become more compassionate towards them. Love as an energy seeks expression and so we focus on helping others or the planet. Here spiritual service work becomes a passion and a motivation. We want to help others in healing ways or simply as a friend.

A person operating from this level of consciousness has a strong healing presence. By being in their physical presence, it is possible to feel the divine energies and consciousness they embody. This healing works principally in opening the hearts of others. It uplifts, heals and expands the energies of others.

Common Challenges

When we enter into a new level of consciousness, many aspects of ourselves change. Our thoughts, feelings, motivations and energies change from what they used to be. It becomes necessary to adjust to these changes and challenges often emerge in this process. The most common challenge is to learn how to be comfortable experiencing unconditional love. Most people have experienced a more common form of love such as with a romantic love with a partner or as in the love between a parent and child. Most people are familiar with this and expect all of their loving feelings to be focused on this select group of people. However unconditional love is a state of consciousness where we experience loving thoughts and feelings for most people and often with complete strangers. We may have feelings of appreciation for others and a desire to help them. There may be feelings of connection and attraction which defy normal explanation. There can be a tendency to misunderstand these feelings and especially when they come about from our interactions with those people who might have previously represented potential romantic partners. Here these feelings of connection may be misinterpreted as romantic feelings. It is certainly true that in lower levels of consciousness feelings of attraction are most often experienced exclusively in romantic relationships, however with unconditional love these feelings of connection represent new and different experiences of love. We can still have romantic relationships in crystal consciousness but we need to be skilled at noticing the differences between genuine romantic feelings and feelings of connection and attraction to others that comes about through our experience of spiritual love or unconditional love. Here we can monitor our thoughts and feelings in such situations in order to challenge our initial assumptions. The word unconditional indicates that we can have loving feelings for others without requiring them to do anything for us or behave in any particular way. We do not expect or desire romantic relationships from others but appreciate this spiritual love for what it is.

Another challenging situation may come about with those relationships where the loving spiritual connections and attraction are most felt. These are very often with likeminded spiritual people who operate at higher levels of consciousness. These individuals have the ability to amplify the loving experiences of unconditional love. The experience of such relationships can be uplifting, fulfilling and exquisite. Very often we greatly value these relationships and the experiences that they bring. These close friendships bring relief from less satisfying relationships and we may want to perpetually enjoy them. Very often this is not possible for practical reasons. We must appreciate these moments and experiences for what they bring to us without wishing to cling to them. Here we realise that we can experience many such moments as our energies attract these potentials to us. We do not have to force these situations into being. They can simply flow into our experience.

Existing Crystals and Ghost Crystals

There are those older souls who have achieved Crystal Consciousness in previous lifetimes. As such this level becomes their "default" setting in this lifetime. This is the level of consciousness that they feel most comfortable being and so they have every potential to achieve this again in this lifetime. To exist at the level of Crystal Consciousness one needs to have an open heart and express unconditional love in everyday life. However daily life offers frequent challenges for all of us and it is common for sensitive people to find these harsh. Often they close down their hearts after experiencing emotional pain in order to protect themselves from further pain. This is of course the wrong course of action as it shuts down higher consciousness itself but is a common response and many crystals experience this. Please remember that we can lower our level of personal consciousness as well as can raise it. This reaction of closing the heart to avoid emotional pain often does not a result from conscious decision to do way. It is more like an emotional reaction that bypasses the mind. The closing down of the heart in a crystal results in a Ghost Crystal. They limit their interactions with the world around them and withdraw from life. They become a shadow of themselves as they hide their true beauty and power and become ghost like. Their potentials to operate in higher consciousness still remain but will be dormant until they open their hearts again. This is the greatest challenge of crystals and is ever present.

The Master Teacher of Crystal level unconditional love is Jesus Christ who taught the way of the heart.

Phase of Crystal Consciousness - Unconditional Joy

Key words: self love, inner divine realisation, introspection, profound gratitude

phase of consciousness	actual experience	key attributes needed	challenges at this level	surrender required for next level
Unconditional Joy	Deep realisation of eternal divine presence within self leading to joyful experience of self and life	Self love, time and space to allow the emerging realisation of divine self	To "divert" loving focus away from outer world to inner world, Learning about non-attachment	Let go of negative thoughts and emotions, embracing divine identity as well as human identity Practicing NON-ATTACHMENT

Although the level of unconditional joy is similar to the unconditional love level, it is more expansive. The previous level of unconditional love was an outwards focus but unconditional joy is more of an inner focus. Loving expressions do not cease but time and energy are diverted to the inner experience as well now.

Joy includes the deep realisation that the source of love and connection to the divine lies inside of each of us. It is felt as an expansion in the top part of the chest or higher heart.

This is an Inner journey where we discover the divine presence within us. We realise that we are a part of God / Goddess and always have been. Profound joy comes about as we realise that what we have been searching for in the external world was always and will always be present inside of us.

A being of joy

A "joy" will radiate out their spirituality as an unseen and powerful energy. They will show themselves to be in two worlds at once. Whilst operating in the physical world they are also interacting with the unseen worlds of spiritual dimensions. Others will sense these spiritual connections in a Joy even though they may not be able to explain how they are aware of this.

The theme of Joy is non-attachment. From an observers point of view a person practising non-attachment stands out from normal people. They seem to be somewhat removed from normal human emotions and thinking. They are calmer and respond to situations instead of reacting to them. A joy will use more expanded and philosophical understandings of their life. This may seem as if they do not care about themselves of others. However this sense of non attachment is really a reflection of a higher way of being in operation. A joy still cares but in a higher consciousness way. Those who have achieved higher consciousness themselves will recognise this in a joy. Non-attachment as a way of being was taught by Siddhartha Gautama Buddha around the time of c. 563 BCE to 483 BCE. His teachings became the foundation for Buddhism. As such I have nominated him as the Master of Crystal consciousness Joy.

Identification as experienced within the Crystal levels of human consciousness

A Crystal level being identifies with the unseen worlds and dimensions of spiritual energies and realities as perceived through their inner senses and revealed by their soul. Here less importance is placed on the intellectual experience of spirituality. Identification is now switching from the intellectual relationship to the world to experiences of connection to people and the world at large. This is brought about through a soul infused emotional reconnection to life experienced as a pure and growing love of all things. "I" becomes not just a physical being experiencing spirituality through the intellect, but also a being remembering a universal love that is the essence of the soul and remembering how this allows the experience of oneness. In relation to the world around us, "I" appears to be an individual but this identity becomes more blurred as "I" is also exists as Universal Love. Universal Love brings us the realisation of a way being and belonging that is outside of the body, thoughts and personality. Universal love at this level of consciousness is still focused mainly in the physical world with a sense of kinship with people, acknowledgement of the loving support of the divine in our life as well as an appreciation of beauty, mystery and magnificence of the physical world.

How transcendence of the negative ego is experienced within Crystal Consciousness unconditional love leading to Unconditional Joy

With universal acceptance we are free to appreciate life without needing to confront or change it. We start to notice its beauty and the divine perfection in all things that was once hidden from our awareness. We fall in love with life. The great struggles of the Indigo phase are let go and we feel a new lightness and it is enjoyable. Gratitude grows within us for this new found freedom. We extend love to all things and this becomes natural.

Love of course is the opposite of fear. Whilst we are experiencing love as our reality we have fundamentally disarmed the negative ego. This is a powerful transformational experience as the worst experiences of the negative ego are less common as long as this loving focus is maintained. We are aware of the wonder and profundity of the world around us and we become humble in its awesome presence. The negative ego is further diminished in this way as it is hard for it to influence us towards negativity and conflict if we maintain a loving and humble nature. The negative ego projects a grandiose self image and seeks conflict. Both of these are as less likely to happen in the unconditional love state of being. As long as we experience this level of love as our reality we have disarmed the negative ego but we have not fully transcended it. The negative ego remains as a dormant potential held in place but it is possible for any individual to descend in consciousness to lower levels if the loving focus is abandoned. Transcending the negative ego comes when we operate from out Universal Awareness and in its presence the negative ego is dissolved.

Within the sense of wonder that is the Crystal Consciousness experience, we start to notice an expanded level of awareness which is our universal awareness. We become aware of awareness itself. This often happens in periods of meditation or contemplation when we are not distracted by a busy mind and the activity of thinking. There are special qualities to these experiences which are profound and mystical. These include a peace and a sense of unlimited potential. We experience pure knowing as opposed to thoughts and thinking. The most startling realisation is that this part of us is eternal and has always been available to us. It is just that we did not notice it before. It is normal for us to seek out deeper experiences of Universal Awareness and so we allow ourselves to merge with it in meditation and also when we day dream. There is no perceptual limit to Universal Awareness. Whatever we desire to connect with, the Universal awareness gives us a focused awareness of this. The feelings of freedom and belonging this gives us makes us feel complete. These are the experiences that many have been unconsciously searching for and so this is a coming home experience. Of course we are coming home when we are aware of our Universal Awareness as this is an eternal part of us that existed before the creation of our ego and personality.

The tendency within Crystal Consciousness is to see the wonder in others. It is mainly an outwards expression of love. This is a positive movement of consciousness however it leads us to a new core spiritual agenda of allowing some of this love and wonder to be directed to our self. This is the journey of self love. Many find this a hard task. The insecurity of the negative ego and its fear of rejection bring about a self loathing and a sense of unworthiness. Society declares that self love is merely vanity and the expression of an egotist. The world view is that we have no value unless we are beautiful, rich or talented. However all of these things are illusions just as the negative ego is the biggest illusion of all. When we truly experience our Universal Awareness as divine consciousness we realise that we are a part of the divine and that the divine is not exclusively found outside of us. Any unresolved areas in relation to self love are now raised and this becomes the core agenda that leads us into the level of Joy.

Unconditional Joy

At this level the unmistakable realisation we experience is that we are not our thoughts or emotions nor are we the complex workings of the negative ego. We realise that we are primarily the pure consciousness of the Universal Awareness. This brings peace and freedom from the confusion and negativity that is normal in lower states of consciousness where the negative ego has great influence. This freedom brings joy and truth. Joy is not happiness which is temporary and conditional. We are only happy when something happens that brings us satisfaction and often this is short lived. Within joy we recognise that our Universal Awareness cannot be taken away from us and has much more to reveal to us. We find the spiritual power and purpose that we have been unconsciously searching for all along. Joy is unconditional as whatever is happening in our outer life our inner truth and freedom remain present and permanent. We are not dependent on any particular events to occur in our daily life in order that we experience joy. We learn about being non-attached to events in our daily life. These important experiences lead us to a new way of being.

To achieve the level of Joy we must learn to love ourselves at a deep level. If a person feels so unworthy of allowing self-love then how can they allow God to love them? At this level the last remaining issues surrounding self-love are explored and resolved. After experiencing the immense amount of love that God has for us personally, it becomes futile to hang onto negative thoughts about self.

The experience of Joy places us into a new level of consciousness. Here we begin to be in two worlds at once. We are still a part of the physical world and yet we are very much plugged into divine realisations and ways of being. It changes us at every level. One important experience of this is in how we become non-attached to people and events.

Attachment and detachment are polarised approaches to life that most people have. Attachment occurs when we cannot be happy or satisfied unless our wishes are met in specific ways. This approach is prevalent in lower consciousness as there is the basic assumption that what we need exists outside of self and therefore we are dependent on the outside world to bring us happiness, love and meaning into our lives. The attachment to specific outcomes is driven by the fears of the personality and the negative ego.

To be detached from something means that we are trying to avoid it or more accurately we are trying to avoid any discomfort that it brings. Both approaches bring their difficulties.

At the level of Joy we are not so dependent on outer situations, people and events to bring us deep meaning, love and happiness. Why? This is because we are now receiving these things directly from the universe. As such we become less attached to receiving these in everyday life as we see they are no longer so important to us. Being less attached moves us towards non-attachment. And so we commonly feel, "If it happens then great and if it does not then fine!" This attitude is supported by our faith in the divine to look after us and from our own ability to master our thoughts and feelings. We begin to have much broader divine and multi-dimensional perspectives.

The viewpoint of non-attachment is tested when we see others suffering. I know that we can love people AND be non-attached to their suffering. We love them for who they are and not as a result of their suffering. In this state we are aligned to divine energies and wisdom and not aligned to their negative thoughts and energies. It is all about where we align our energies and thoughts. This is because we know that their pain is often a part of their spiritual journey. As such the greatest gift that we can give them is for us to embody divine wisdom and energies so to remind them of their own power to remove themselves from their situation. This is the most empowered gift that we have and indeed this is how the ascended masters work with us. Please imagine if Buddha or Jesus were here on earth. Would they identify with the problem (a person's negativity) or with the solution (divine wisdom and connection)?

When we change our perspective we change how we operate in such situations and become non-attached and free of personal negative experiences. Initially this feels strange as if we are abandoning people. This is because we have been used to gravitating between attached and detached viewpoints which represent two extremes. We do not have to make this choice. To be non-attached removes us from this level of thinking and the need to feel guilty if we do not want to experience their pain.

Progression to Rainbow Consciousness

Crystal consciousness is all about experiencing love. We can love everything in this level. This includes loving our past lives, current life, self, God and all levels of creation. When we have the wisdom to see divine perfection in all that has happened and how this has helped us, we can accept the past. When we love, accept and embrace rather than to judge and criticise things then we can let go of the past and love ourselves free of it. When we have loved everything then we move forwards. We love ourselves free and in Rainbow consciousness we explore that freedom.

Rainbow Consciousness - Multidimensional Exploration

Key words: Mystical, Connected, Multi-dimensional, expanded awareness, peace, & serenity

Key experiences and motivations

Deeply physic, empathic and telepathic

Development of higher senses

Channel of divine energies and consciousness

Highly sensitive to spiritual energies

Deep loss of self as personality (mini deaths)

Brow chakras development and activation

phase of consciousness	actual experience	key attributes needed	challenges at this level	surrender required for next level
Peace	Split awareness between physical plane and higher dimensions	Ability to focus on and master the dimensional "options"	To find balance between "being" and "doing", how to integrate higher consciousness in daily life	To let go of earthly life, the past and large aspects of the personality

Rainbow Consciousness offers unlimited spiritual opportunity if we are prepared to let go of our limited realities. This is a very expansive level of consciousness. The predominate experience at this level is a deep sense of peace and bliss as at this level the negative ego and the concepts of separation have largely been transcended. Without the fear, pain and anxiety that the negative ego promotes in our experience what is left? Profound stillness, universal oneness and perfection of being are experienced. It is peace and serenity which are the natural experiences of higher states of being.

In higher consciousness, we experience altered states of awareness. The normal human "beta" level of awareness becomes too restrictive and boring. We need to spend time in expanded levels in whatever way we can. This could be in meditation or in a type of daydream state where we are simply "being" and not "doing" anything. Within these altered states of consciousness we experience Universal Awareness. We are having multidimensional experiences, meaning we are simultaneously "here" in awareness in the physical dimension as well as being "there" in unseen dimensions of expanded consciousness and experience. Here normal thinking and physical activity become tedious and we resist these. Specifically in Rainbow there is a lot of right brain activity leading to mystical and intuitive experiences. This becomes the normal "default" way of being instead of the typical left brain experiences of logic, structure, verbal communication. Normal left brain activity increasingly feels more boring and difficult. This is normal.

We have to re-program ourselves to understand that these are valid spiritual experiences as the common belief is that we need busy doing things in order to achieve anything. It is especially important that during periods of spiritual growth that we allow ourselves to become accustomed to these new levels of consciousness and being. This is a time of integration of the new energies and levels of awareness. We learn how our physical body, emotions and thoughts respond to this new level.

At these expanded levels of consciousness we become more aware of how we are connected to everything else. We perceive there to be less separation between us and with other people as we can read other people's thoughts and emotions. We interact with people whilst acting as a channel for divine energies and wisdom in daily life. There is the growing appreciation for oneness. It becomes less important for us to express our personality in daily life as we are expressing divine presence more and more. We become less interested in what other people think about spiritual matters as the divine becomes our source of understanding of the world around us and beyond the physical. We recognise common spiritual philosophies and practices do not always fit into the expanded awareness of the Rainbow level of consciousness. The divine connections made available through Rainbow consciousness become our preferred source for information and understanding as they offers much more for us than what fellow spiritual seekers and teachers can offer. As such we find that spiritual books and other people's perceptions generally become less important to us and we see their limitations. Divine connections allow us to receive pure and infinite understanding which is perceived in all ways and not just intellectually. At this level we are much more likely to meditate, contemplate and day dream as a method to access these divine gifts. These are all methods of altering our state of consciousness so that we are more open to the flow of divine connection. Accordingly we tend to read less books and connect less to other people. However it takes time to get accustomed to this new level of reality as it offers its own challenges. We tend to seek our own company and become less sociable. We need more isolation in order to fully experience this higher level of consciousness. At a personality level we have to come to terms with our need for peace and isolation. We may feel guilty as we dedicate more of our time and energy to ourselves and less to other people. If we imagine the stories of sages and gurus of old that lived life styles of quiet solitude then we can appreciate that these personal requirements are part of the way of being of the Rainbow level of consciousness. I am not saying however that it is essential to run off and join a convent, ashram or temple in order to exist at the Rainbow level. It is possible to live in the everyday world at this higher level of consciousness. However it means that we must cater for the new requirements that we will have at this level. We need to find time and space to be alone more and to do those things that bring divine connection which is the fuel of Rainbow consciousness. Certain aspects of life such as relationships, occupation and where we live often have to change as a part of this process.

For a reader who has not experienced the Rainbow levels of consciousness these experiences may sound like alarming! It must be remembered that they are part of the transcendence of the personality which is a normal part of Ascension. As our personality influences our experience of life less and less then we make room for the presence of divine love and wisdom. We are not being robbed our personality but rather we are blending our divine self with the best parts of our personality. The personality will never be totally absent in our human experience as we need some level of ego to operate in the physical world.

In previous levels of consciousness we explored our awareness mainly through our thoughts and emotions. Now in the Rainbow level we use also use our inner senses. They normally not used in everyday life and yet they emerge into our awareness at this level. There are no commonly used descriptions or names for these senses and we experience them in unique and mystical ways. Our Inner Senses detect the non-physical experiences when we connect other dimensions of existence, spiritual energies and higher aspects of self. For example when we experience divine consciousness the major impression that we receive is the deep sense of meaning. Now meaning is not an emotion, but our Inner Senses can detect its presence or the absence of meaning.

Identification as experienced within the Rainbow level of human consciousness

A Rainbow level being identifies with multi dimensional realities including spirit (Universal Awareness). Identification is now switching from the intellectual and the exploration of universal love in the outer world to the inner worlds of mystical experiences, intuition and contemplation (a receptive state of being allowing communication with the divine that leads to illumination, inspiration and revelation). "I" becomes not just a physical, intellectual and loving being, but also a being with a growing awareness of their own connection to unseen dimensions of spiritual realities. In relation to the world around us, "I" appears to be an individual but also exists elsewhere in other dimensions. As such "I" is no longer defined as just being "here" in the physical world but also being "there" in other dimensions. This is a profound change in identification.

How transcendence of the negative ego is experienced within Rainbow

There is a requirement within Rainbow consciousness for everyone to make all final surrenders before entering into Diamond Consciousness. Here I would call this level the end of the process where we need to claim a spiritual identity as a human being. Ironically this was the theme previously as we freed ourselves from the lower consciousness of humanity. In previous levels of ascension we tried to understand why we were different from others and how we could live and serve others here on earth. This process is thoroughly explored in Indigo and Crystal consciousness. We continue with this until the Rainbow level where we are asked to let go of this as well as many human concepts of separation. In Rainbow we are asked simply to "be" without definition, judgement or analysis and to allow this in all of its glory. By doing this we channel, anchor and ground our higher self here on earth. With many ascension seekers there is a long standing need to understand self, to define self and to uncover our gifts and purpose. This is a part of the process of ascension but in Rainbow level now we are being asked to let this go. That process is the journey and in Rainbow we have arrived and it is no longer needed. In essence the previous process is a human process and now we are to be divine as well. The divine does not see itself in human terms and so there is no definition, judgement or analysis. This means in Rainbow the expression of our new expanded consciousness is simply to "be".

Rainbow is a multi dimensional awareness. At this level we become aware of dimensional "options" and these are explored. It is a transient phase leading to Diamond Consciousness or Ascension. It is a journey where we go out into the Universe to remember who we are before deciding on how we will express our newly found enlightenment here on earth in this lifetime. We transcend normal human consciousness. Our human identity and personality is understood as being optional. We increasingly identify with our divine presence. Normal human consciousness and the ego feel boring and restrictive. We want to simply "be" and to enjoy our expanded awareness. It is like a living meditation or day dream but the realizations that we receive are not illusionary. To the contrary we recognize how illusionary normal human consciousness truly is.

The story of Jesus and the forty days and nights spent in the desert presents an insight to the challenges of Rainbow consciousness. For me this story is less about resisting temptation and more about truly finding ourselves in higher consciousness. The forty days and nights for me represents a time when Jesus was challenged to let go of his humanity in order to further embrace his divinity. Naturally there is resistance in all of us to this process. It is human nature to cling onto that which is known and for the ego to protect its limited identity. Even Jesus struggled against his human nature. In Rainbow we are invited to let go of so much which we once identified with so strongly. Our sense of separateness, our assumptions about who we are and why we are on earth are all challenged. It is hard to continue to hold ourselves in limitation. We sense our true power and purpose more clearly than ever before. Doubts and questions are raised. We know how perfect, pure and magnificent the divine is. We sense that the divine can flow through us into this world in unimaginable ways. And so the questions that emerge are: How magnificent will I allow myself (our self) to be? How much will I surrender to the divine and simply be divine expression in this world? These are inconceivable questions for our minds and yet we sense these new emerging realities. This is not a question of ego. We are not talking about how we may benefit from being an agent of the divine. We doubt that we can truly represent the divine in an authentic way. Can I truly be divine?! Any unresolved feelings of unworthiness and self love are finally challenged here.

My own experiences of Rainbow are that this is a challenging period on all levels. Energetically we are changed profoundly. We are rewired so that we are merged with vast energy fields.

The brow chakra is strongly activated. The influence of these changes works in exponential ways. If for example Indigo is represented by 1 in terms of spiritual consciousness then maybe Crystal is 10 and Rainbow 100. I remember at times feeling absolutely exhausted and needing just to be still and rest. These are periods of integrating energetic changes at a physical level. I suffered from migraine headaches as my third eye was active. This chakra became very sensitive as at times it was overloaded with stimulation. Emotionally it is a tough ride too. In Rainbow the final battles between our ego and divine intention take place. It is the time of the deepest transcendence of ego. Any difficult and unresolved issues surface at this time and demand our attention. The universe expertly provides the people and situations to help us with this! Our emotions reflect this process and we feel agitated, frustrated and generally uncomfortable. Often we are not consciously aware of the themes of these internal battles taking place in our psyche. How ironic it is that in our periods of greatest spiritual achievement we feel so terrible!

At a conscious level our understandings are challenged. We become aware of other expanded realities and therefore have to give up old assumptions of how things are. We increasingly see through the illusions of humanity and so become more distanced from those people who continue to operate from lower consciousness.

In rainbow we revise our thoughts about our life missions. This is natural as we have more insight shaping our views.

The Master Teacher of Rainbow level is Mary Magdalene. This was a Master who embodied the magical qualities of Rainbow consciousness. She was a portal to other realms and dimensions which others accessed simply by being in her presence. She taught about Universal Truth and especially the Divine Feminine in a humble fashion and free of ego. Her communication was not so much verbal as through her presence and her energies.

Diamond Consciousness -
Divine Exploration and Expression
Key experiences and motivations

Surrender to Divine at all levels
Acceptance of the purpose for divine union
Transcendence of negative ego, personality, humanity and the physical universe
Mastery of thought, emotions and energy
Service to divine & humanity

Phases of Diamond Consciousness

Transcendence

Key words: The Master, Mastery, Transcendence, Service

phase of conscious-ness	actual experience	key attributes needed	challenges at this level	surrender required for next level
Transcendence	Living in divine flow and grace having achieved mastery of self and divine surrender and divine union	Constantly seeking balance and to maintain higher consciousness	To be a spiritual leader through mastery and service work, operating at a different level of consciousness to virtually everyone else	To be non-attached to all aspects of human experience and living, to say "goodbye" to earth, humanity and personal human identity

The Diamond level is the ascended state of consciousness where the negative ego has been mostly transcended. We have surrendered at all levels and transcended the negative ego in favour of our spirit. Here the personality allows the spirit to flow through us without resistance. We have mastered our own human condition so that our emotions, thoughts and action reflect our desire to simply "be" the full expression of universal awareness rather than to reflect the normal and dysfunctional patterns of humanity. We become Ascended Masters in waiting and are able to fully anchor our life missions and spiritual gifts. We channel our spirit and divine love, wisdom and presence. At the Diamond level we are fully aligned to divine service. Hence service work is the theme of Diamond Consciousness.

At a broader level the Diamond level is where we merge with vast and expansive fields of energy and consciousness. These are at the Galactic levels and include alignment with the Galactic Centre which is the focal point of highest levels of divine connection and purpose in the Galaxy. The Galactic centre is also a portal to other Galaxies, Universes and dimensions of consciousness. As such the Diamond being is over lighted by the vast intelligence and activity of the Galactic centre. A Diamond being expresses its divine purpose with their presence and within service work. These energy fields also include that which is called the Christ Consciousness. This is the aspect of the divine intelligence that seeks expression in this physical world. As such it is an energy that inspires us to put our spirituality into motion and to serve earth and humanity. This service is often expressed as spiritual teaching and hence the phrase "The Christ" is often used in connection to World Teachers such as Jesus and Buddha.

At this level of being, the symbol of the Diamond is used to recognise how many facets or aspects of self have been perfected.

Identification as experienced within the Diamond levels of human consciousness

A Diamond level being identifies with spirit and the expression of spirit in this world. They are not just exploring their connections to universal awareness but they are also expressing them. "I" is not just a multi dimensional being aware of its condition in a somewhat passive way, but becomes consciously active in aligning itself with universal awareness and finding ways to channel this in the physical world.

How transcendence of the negative ego is experienced within Diamond Consciousness

It is not just the negative ego that has been transcended but all aspects of human being. This includes our personality, our relationships, humanity itself and the planet earth. In a sense we say "goodbye" to these things as we no longer identify with them as much as before. They are no longer represent our sense of our "home" to which we belong to. This does not mean that we no longer care about or love these things. It means that we no longer identify with being just human and these things do not have such a hold on us as before. We are truly non-attached to such things. We are not losing these aspects. They are still there but we are embracing a more multi-dimensional reality in which they command less of our attention and we place less importance on them.

At this level we have even transcended the desires of the soul. This allows the being to be free of earthly attachments and karma. Our desires are no longer personal but divine in the sense that they are aligned to divine and therefore seek to express divine meaning and purpose rather than the interests of the personality.

Phases of Diamond Consciousness - Completion

Key words: Climax, Ecstasy, Union, Oneness

Completion

The Diamond level describes an Ascended Master in waiting. Such a being has the awareness and qualities of an Ascended Master but they have not reached the conclusion of their ascension which is called COMPLETION. Completion is the climax to the ascension process where the pure and full force of their spirit merges with all other aspects of self. This profound event is beyond the ability of words to describe. It is the conclusion of many life times where a being merges back into oneness and returns in awareness to source and truly remembers its reason for being created. It is a declaration of that being to the universe expressing its love for life itself and gratitude for its creation. It is a celebration of source by the ascended masters as they lose all remaining illusions and truly realises that they are source itself. This event can last only a few seconds or minutes. It can be at the point of physical death but this is not necessary. The point of completion is more than the personal triumph of Ascension. The experience of the completion of ascension is shared with all creation as it anchors spirit into the many levels of creation in deeper ways. The expression, "bringing heaven to earth" really does describe this point of completion.

The master teachers of Diamond levels are those beings and teachers who form aspects of the spiritual hierarchy such as the Maha Chohan and the Christ (Maitreya). There are also group or universal energies and intelligence that guides us in the Diamond level from the Galactic Core and star groups.

Lightning Source UK Ltd.
Milton Keynes UK
17 February 2011

167674UK00002B/1/P

9 781450 273800